COLLECTIBLE

Collectible Cups & Saucers

BOOK II

COLLECTOR BOOKS
A Division of Schroeder Publishing Co., Inc.

ON THE COVER

Snack set. Limoges, T. & V., artist signed R. Mills, c. 1892 – 1907.
Art Nouveau Persian decoration. $100.00 – 125.00.

Cover design: Beth Summers
Book design: Sherry Kraus

Collector Books
P.O. Box 3009
Paducah, KY 42002-3009

The current values in this book should be used only as a guide. They are not intended to set prices, which vary from one section of the country to another. Auction prices as well as dealer prices vary greatly and are affected by condition as well as demand. Neither the authors nor the publisher assumes responsibility for any losses which might be incurred as a result of consulting this guide.

CONTENTS

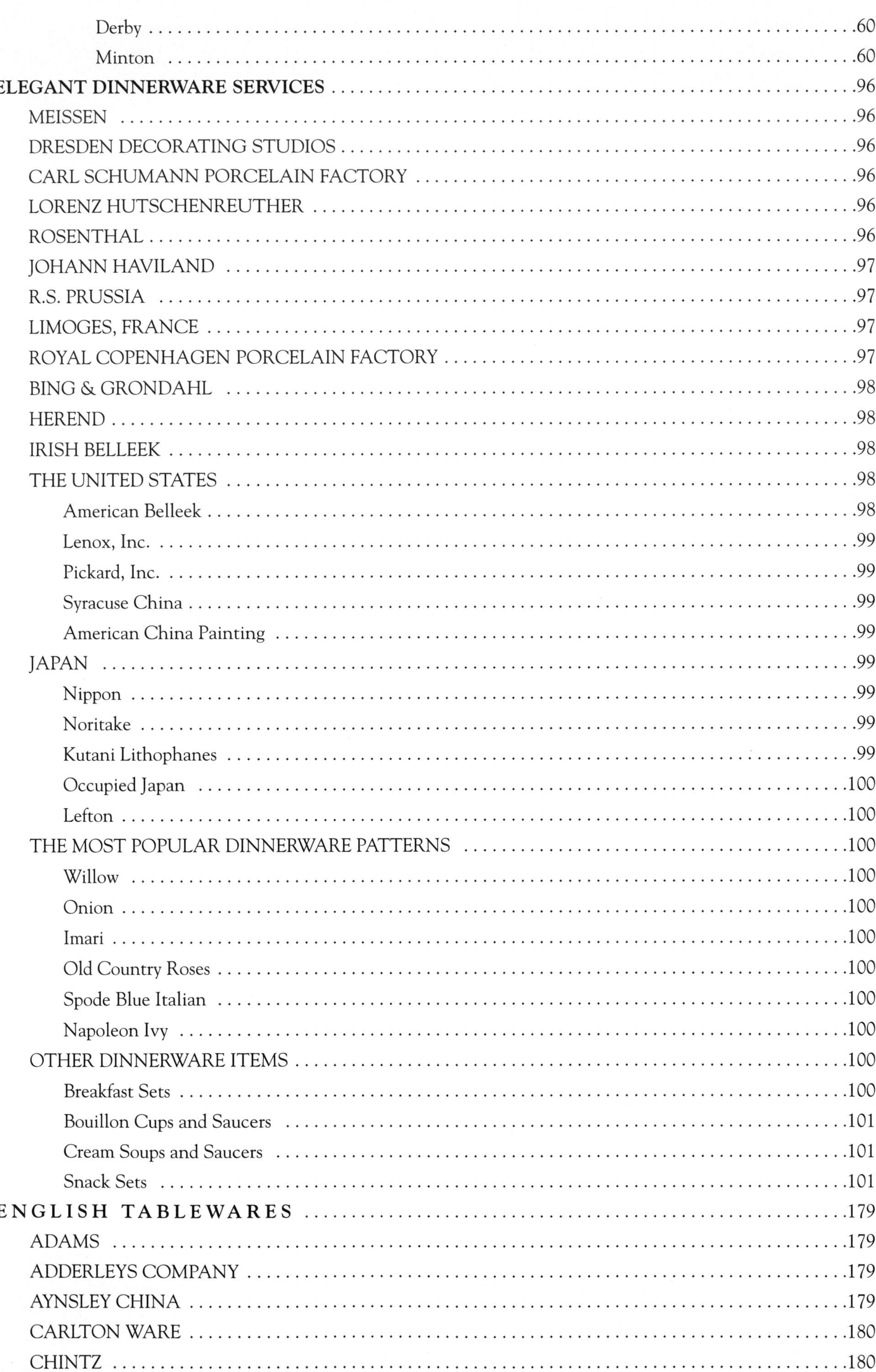

DEDICATION

To Michael and Linda, Jeff and Joyce,
Stan and Maxine, and Edward

ABOUT THE AUTHORS

Susan and Jim Harran, antique dealers for 18 years, specialize in English and Continental porcelains and antique cups and saucers. The Harrans write feature articles for various antique publications and have a monthly column in *AntiqueWeek*, entitled "The World of Ceramics." Susan is a member of the Antique Appraisal Association of America, Inc. The Harrans enjoy traveling around the country to keep abreast of trends in the antiques marketplace. They reside in Neptune, New Jersey.

ACKNOWLEDGMENTS

We would like to express our appreciation to those collectors and dealers who so generously gave of their time and knowledge to make this book a reality. We are indebted to Richard Gidman of Dainty Blue Antiques, North Truro, Massachusetts, for sending us over 200 pictures from his wonderful collection of Shelley and Titian Ware cups and saucers. We realize the time and effort involved and are deeply grateful for his help.

A special thank you to Marguerite Verley of New Lenox, Illinois, for once again sharing her extensive knowledge of early British cups and saucers with us. The lovely photographs from her collection were taken by Olin F. Taylor. Marguerite is writing a book on British tableware and recently went to England to research her book. We wish her well in her endeavor.

We would like to thank Richard W. Kipperman of Grantham, New Hampshire, for his contributions to our new mustache cups and saucers section. Richard sent us over 20 photographs from his spectacular collection.

Thanks to Sharon Cobb of San Diego, California, for sending us so many excellently researched photographs from her wonderful cup and saucer collection. We appreciate the professional quality of her photographs.

We appreciate the many fine photographs from Brenda and Don Pardee of Bloomville, New York. The Pardees have a large collection of cups and saucers in a variety of styles and forms.

We thank Carol Benjamin who has given us a standing invitation to visit her in New Paltz, New York, for a cup of tea. Not only did Carol send us lovely pictures from her collection, but she took the time to draw some of the marks to help in our research.

A special thanks to Nancy Hurd of Copley, Ohio, for her contribution of photographs from her wonderful English bone china cup and saucer collection. The quality of her photographs are excellent and much appreciated.

Our appreciation is extended to Linda Richards of Temple, Texas, for once again volunteering photographs from her interesting demitasse collection. We appreciate her enthusiasm toward our endeavors.

Special thanks to Richard Rendall of Cincinnati, Ohio, for sharing his extensive knowledge and love of hand-painted porcelain. Thanks to Kathleen Digan of San Jose, California; Edie Hustvedt of Annapolis, Maryland; Chris and Mercy Sutton from North Miami, Florida; Frances Pryor of Greenfield, Indiana; Elaine McAllister from Clarksville, Tennessee; Lorraine Schaeffer from Henrietta, New York; Elaine L. Weil from Fort Campbell, Kentucky; Bernadette M. White from Frederick, Maryland; and Steven Goss of Yaxley, England, for contributing photographs of cups and saucers from their collections. We appreciate the time spent photographing and researching them.

We appreciate Mark Brown and Tim Sublette of Seekers Antiques, Columbus, Ohio, for allowing us to come into their booth during an antique show and photograph 13 rare and early English cups and saucers.

Thanks to the late Susan Weitzen, New York, for giving us permission to take photographs of her Wedgwood collection.

We would like to express our sincere appreciation to Pickard Inc., Antioch, Illinois, for sending us photographs illustrating the making of a cup.

Thanks to our Internet friend, Charlene Margiotta, for her excellent illustrations of cup and saucer shapes and handles. Charlene is a professional commercial artist and can be reached at Margiotta Studio, 149 South Middletown Rd., Nanuet, NY, 10965, 914-624-2426.

Lastly, we again thank Todd Robertson, owner of Shore Service Photo in Neptune City, New Jersey, and members of his staff, Barbara and Marie, for their support in our challenging task of photographing over 800 cups and saucers.

PREFACE

Antique dealers for 18 years, we specialize in fine Continental and English porcelains, with emphasis on antique cups and saucers. An infinite variety of cups and saucers are available for both the new and experienced collector, and they can be found in all price ranges. There is probably no better way to thoroughly know and understand the various ceramic manufacturers than to study cups and saucers.

In our research on cups and saucers, we were surprised to find that, other than Michael Berthoud's *A Compendium of British Cups* and Garth Clark's *The Book of Cups*, there are no other books in print available on cups and saucers, specifically. In order to fairly price our merchandise, it has been necessary to dig through general price guides and auction catalogs, as well as to observe the prices on similar pieces at shows and shops, to try to determine realistic prices. Many of our customers have asked us if there is a resource available to help them learn about cups and saucers.

We realized there was a need for a book about collectible cups and saucers and decided to write one.

Our first edition, *Collectible Cups and Saucers Identification and Values*, was published by Collector Books in 1997, and values were updated in 1999. We are very pleased with the success of the book. We are receiving unsolicited comments from readers who have bought the book, and the response has been 100% favorable. Collectors tell us our book is very helpful, and ask when we are going to write another one. We've had many offers of help.

We are observing a tremendous increase of activity in the buying and selling of cups and saucers at antique shows, in our shop, and especially on the Internet. On one popular auction site, over 400 individual cups and saucers are listed daily. Collectors tell us they not only display their cups and saucers in their homes, but enjoy using them.

There is an almost endless variety of cups and saucers in the marketplace. For this reason, we decided to write a second book. Again, our purpose has been to concentrate on actual cups and saucers that are readily available rather than museum pieces; therefore, all of the 800+ photographs in this book were taken from cups and saucers that have been in our inventory, those from other dealers, or from private collections.

The purpose of this book is to provide, all in one source, historical information on tea, coffee, hot chocolate, early cup and saucer forms and shapes, and how cups and saucers were made and decorated. We have added illustrations on cup shapes and handles, photographs depicting various decorative techniques, and pictures demonstrating the manufacturing process. We include a brief history of the most popular manufacturers, a representative sample of their products, and what we hope is a realistic price range.

We've included some helpful information for collectors, early catalog reprints, and an all new section on commonly found marks.

We have divided the book into six collecting categories, although they overlap, and many collectors enjoy examples from each. The first group is a representative collection of early cups and saucers dating from the 1700s until 1875.

The second group, dedicated to the advanced collector, is cabinet cups — those exquisite works of art that are too fragile and costly to be used. Because true cabinet cups and saucers are so rare and usually found in museums and private collections, we have taken the liberty to include cups and saucers that we think are especially fine, even though we know they were once part of a tea or coffee set and made to be used.

The third category, late nineteenth and twentieth century dinnerware, is by far the

largest and the foundation of most collections. In this group we have included tea, coffee, demitasse, and chocolate cups and saucers from many companies in Europe, Japan, and the United States.

A fourth group that is growing in popularity is the lovely twentieth century English bone china and pottery cups and saucers. They are abundant and the prices are reasonable, making them perfect for the beginner to collect. We also discuss the Shelley and Chintz phenomena, Adams Titian Ware, Carlton Ware, and the increased popularity of Aynsley China.

The fifth popular category is miniatures. Although these tiny gems were made as early as the seventeenth century, they are as elusive as "a needle in a haystack," and prices are soaring.

Our brand new sixth section introduces mustache cups and saucers. These fascinating treasures from a bygone era are also difficult to find. We've noticed increased interest in this category.

There are several other media or cup forms that we have not addressed in this book simply because we had to draw the line somewhere. An entire book could be written about glass cups and saucers, as well as souvenir and coronation collectibles.

Many publications and ceramic manufacturers supplied helpful information, and these sources are acknowledged in the bibliography. Hopefully, this book will make it easier for the beginning, as well as the advanced collector, dealer, and appraiser, to identify and price cups and saucers. We realize that in a book of this nature and scope, some degree of error is unavoidable, and we apologize in advance.

We would appreciate hearing your comments, and our address is below. If you would like a reply, please include a self-addressed stamped envelope.

SUSAN AND JIM HARRAN
208 Hemlock Drive
Neptune, NJ 07753

"Mishap at cat's tea party." Melissa Klasik Kards, London.

EARLY DEVELOPMENT

THE HISTORY OF TEA

"Thank God for tea! What would the world do without tea? How did it exist? I am glad I was not born before tea." (Lady Holland's Memoirs)

The story of tea began in ancient China over 5,000 years ago. Legend has it that the Emperor Shen-Nong, a skillful ruler and scientist, was boiling his drinking water as a health precaution, and some leaves from a nearby tree were blown into the pot, imparting a delicate flavor. From that point on, the Emperor ordered the tea leaves to be put in his water all the time.

Tea became China's national drink during the eighth century, and it was called ch'a. It was introduced to Japan in 805 A.D. by a Buddhist priest who had previously visited China. By the fifteenth century tea drinking in Japan became a traditional and important ceremony called cha-no-yu.

The ships of the East India Company regularly sailed to China and introduced the exotic drink of tea to Europe. One of the earliest mentions of tea on the Continent is in the 1615 expense account of an East India Company official. He itemizes: "Three silver porringers to drink chaw in." Jesuit priests traveling on the ships are said to have brought the tea drinking habits back to Portugal. The first was Father Jasper de Cruz in 1560.

When introduced to France about 1660, tea aroused a lively controversy. Balzac said women who drink tea are "pale, sickly, talkative, boring and preachy." Others believed tea stimulated the mind. Louis XIV's physician, Lé Mery, wrote in 1702 that if limited to 10 or 12 cups per day, tea refreshed spirits and cured headaches.

Thomas Garvay was among the first merchants to trade tea in Britain. He offered tea in dry and liquid forms at his coffee house in London's Exchange Alley, holding his first public sale in 1657. The first recorded tea advertisement announcing the sale of "China tcha, tay or tee" appeared in 1658 in the *Mercurius Politicus* newspaper, written by the owner of the Sultaness Head Coffee House.

Tea drinking quickly caught on in England. Two pounds, two ounces of tea were presented to Charles II by the East India Company in 1660. Tea importation rose from 40,000 pounds in 1699 to an average annual consumption of 240,000 pounds by 1708. Today, tea is the national drink of Great Britain, with over 20 million cups of tea served daily in London alone.

Peter Stuyvesant brought the first tea to the colonists in America in New Amsterdam (later named New York by the English). Settlers there became confirmed tea drinkers, and it caught on all across the colonies. Feelings about tea changed in 1773 when the infamous Boston Tea Party occurred. Thirty to 60 men, disguised as Indians, boarded ships owned by the British East India Company. Once aboard, they smashed open tea cargoes from wooden chests and threw them overboard as a protest against massive taxation of the colonies. Every patriotic American gave up tea drinking and turned to coffee.

POPULAR TEA GARDENS

Tea gardens originated in Holland in the 1680s. Dutch inn and tavern owners provided guests with a portable tea set and heating unit. The guests would then prepare tea for themselves and their friends outside in the garden.

English travelers to Holland brought home news of the Dutch "tavern gardens." Soon tea gardens opened all over England with tea being served as the high point of the afternoon. It was at such a tea garden that Lord Nelson, who defeated Napoleon at sea, met the great love of his life, Emma, who became Lady Hamilton. Women were permitted to enter into a mixed, public gathering for the first time without social criticism. Dancing was included, so from tea gardens came the idea of the tea dance, which remained fashionable in England until World War II.

THE JOYS OF AFTERNOON TEA

"There are few hours in life more agreeable than the hours dedicated to the ceremony known as afternoon tea." (Henry James, *Portrait of a Lady)*

The English tradition of afternoon tea may never have become the delightful custom it is if it had not been for Anna, the seventh Duchess of Bedford, in the early part of the ninteenth century. The Duchess, who had a big appetite and was unable to wait for her evening meal, took to her bedroom in the afternoon and had a plate of food with some tea. She often invited friends to join her in her rooms at Belvoir Castle. This practice of inviting friends to come for tea in the afternoon was quickly picked up by other social hostesses, and the afternoon tea was born.

"Nope, I can't drink out of a cup, th' spoon gits in m' eye." Postcard by Twelvetrees, c. 1910.

"The Great Atlantic and Pacific Tea Company's Celebrated Teas and Coffees have been my solace through life." Grandmother Trade Card, c. 1900.

THE HISTORY OF COFFEE

"Ah, how sweet coffee tastes! Lovelier than a thousand kisses, sweeter than muscatel wine! I must have coffee." (*Kaffe Kartate* by Johann Sebastian Bach in 1732)

It is believed the coffee plant was discovered about a thousand years ago in Ethiopia. A shepherd, noticing his sheep were acting lively at night and not sleeping much, spent a few nights observing their behavior. The shepherd noticed the sheep were eagerly eating the blossoms and fruit of a plant he had never noticed before. Trying the food himself, the shepherd became so animated his friends thought he was drunk. When he told them of his discovery they all agreed it was a gift from God and should be enjoyed.

Coffee has been brewed since the fifteenth century in Arabia, often keeping monks awake during their long prayer services. The priests believed the coffee was like liquor and tried to forbid it, but the coffee habit spread all over Arabia and neighboring countries. In Turkey in the fifteenth century it became legal for a woman to divorce her husband if he failed to provide her with her daily coffee quota.

By the early sixteenth century Turkish merchants transported coffee from Arabia to Constantinople, where the first coffee shop was called Kiva Han. Coffee reached Europe about 1585 when Venetian traders brought it to Italy. It fell under harsh criticism from the Catholic church, and many felt the Pope should ban coffee, calling it the "drink of the devil." To everyone's surprise, the Pope, already a coffee drinker, blessed coffee.

In Germany, Frederick the Great regarded coffee as a noble drink and tried to limit it to the court. To emphasize its aristocratic nature he brewed it with champagne.

The Dutch presented a coffee tree to Louis XIV of France. His love of a good cup of coffee led him to build the first greenhouse to nurture his beloved tree. He enjoyed brewing coffee over an alcohol lamp for his intimate friends.

In the 1700s coffee found its way to America by means of a French infantry captain who nurtured one small plant all the way across the Atlantic. This one plant, transplanted to Martinique, became the predecessor of over 19 million trees on the island within 50 years. After the Boston Tea Party, America became a coffee drinking nation, consuming 25 times as much coffee as tea.

"Dilworth's Coffee is unequaled."
Trade card, J.S. Nugent & Co., NY, c. 1900.

"Dilworth's Coffee is unequaled."
Trade card, J.S. Nugent & Co., NY, c. 1900.

Coffee Cup trade card,
Richmond's Cafe,
New Bedford, MA, c. 1910.

COFFEE HOUSES FLOURISHED

Once coffee was introduced to Europe, coffee houses sprang up all over Europe. In England the first coffee house appears to have been opened in Oxford in 1650. People flocked to it to try the new, hot drink they had read about in travel books. Coffee houses sprang up, exclusively for men. They were called "Penny Universities," because for a penny any man could buy a can of coffee and a copy of the newspaper and discuss the news of the day. Coffee was served in a "can" — a straight-sided cup — and poured into a dish, or saucer, for drinking. A tip, "To Insure Promptness," was put in a box, thus starting a custom that has endured to this day.

Coffee houses had a number of other uses, serving as political meeting houses, marriage bureaus, insurance offices, early post offices, and gaming houses. In England the renowned Lloyd's of London Insurance Company got its start inside a coffee house. In the United States at the Merchants Coffee House in New York in 1738, it is said that plans for the American Revolution were discussed.

THE HISTORY OF HOT CHOCOLATE

South American Indians have grown cocoa trees for over a thousand years. It is said the Aztec Indians valued the cocoa bean so much that they used it both in drinks and as a unit of currency.

Columbus was said to have brought a few beans back to Spain after his voyage to South America in 1498. Soon Spanish explorers began to export cocoa beans to Spain and other European countries. Factories were built to make a drinking chocolate, and by the middle of the seventeenth century the drink had spread throughout western Europe.

Drinking chocolate was made by drying cocoa beans and roasting them over a fire. They were pounded to a paste with water and sometimes powdered flowers. By the end of the sixteenth century sugar was added.

"I always drink Huyler's Cocoa or Chocolate!" Huyler's Trade Card, c. 1893.

THE EVOLUTION OF THE CUP

In *The Book of Cups*, Garth Clark observes that history has not been fair to the cup, "...while vases, urns, and teapots have been extolled by poets, painters, and musicians, there has been, for instance, no Ode to a Grecian Cup." He says that we take for granted one of the most useful items at the dinner table.

The cup has a long and fascinating history. Clark says, "It must have been a momentous day when our ancestors discovered that instead of plunging their heads into the streams, they could bring water to their mouth in the cups of their hands." Soon cups were fashioned from leaves, gourds, and woven fibers.

The ceramic cup originated about 8,000 years ago when man learned that putting clay into fire would harden it. The Mycenaeans living in Cyprus in 1100 B.C. drank from cups having the same form as today's modern design. Potters in the Minoan cultures even fashioned miniature cups for their children.

The ancient Greeks copied the cups from the Mycenaean and Minoan cultures and gave them classical beauty. An example is the kylix, a saucer-shaped vessel on an elegant pedestal foot with two handles, which was made in 500 B.C. Water and wine were served in the kylix, and it was held by the bottom. The handles were only used to hang up the cup, and because they were stored in this way, the bases were often beautifully decorated.

In China there have been an infinite variety of tea bowls since the eighth century when tea became a popular beverage. In the Sung Dynasty (960 – 1279 A.D.), bowls were made out of stoneware with a variety of glazes. At the same time, the Chinese were making a type of pottery vastly superior to any seen before. This wonderful new product became known in Europe as "china," or "porcelain," and was first seen when the ships of the East India Companies brought cargo back from China in the 1600s.

The beautiful blue and white porcelain teapots and tea bowls attracted immediate attention. This lovely china became a status symbol, and tea and coffee drinking provided an opportunity for people to show off their wealth with glamorous imported china. It became very common for nobility to pose for portraits holding their favorite cups and saucers. Some individuals carried their personal tea bowls and saucers in special leather and satin carrying cases.

The cup became a very popular icon in the late 1800s due to the increased popularity of tea and coffee drinking and because it symbolized home and hearth. It became one of the most popular themes of postcards, and trade cards in the shape of cups were used by tea, coffee, and chocolate manufacturers. Garth Clark in *The Book of Cups* says, "The symbolic use of the cup has continued into the present day and is the universal sign for refreshment and can be seen on coffee and tea shop signs throughout the world."

"The mere chink of cups and saucers turns the mind to happy repose."

(George Gissie, date unknown)

THE FORMS

TEA BOWLS AND CUPS

The earliest utensils for tea drinking were small porcelain and stoneware bowls imported from China by the East Indian Company in the early seventeenth century. European and English tea bowls imitating Chinese and Japanese originals were produced in stoneware, earthenware, and porcelain from the early eighteenth century onward and were often decorated with chinoiserie or Chinese-type motifs.

In use, the tea bowl presented a problem, especially when the bowl was as small as the early ones. The bowl became very hot and could only be held by the finger and thumb by grasping the top rim and foot rim. The thumb could be placed under the foot and the finger on the rim, but the bowl couldn't be set down in this position. For those drinkers with steady hands, it could be taken to the mouth on the

saucer. Tea bowls did not present a problem for the Chinese as they drank their tea lukewarm.

In the eighteenth century the rather rare handled teacups were, as a rule, only supplied with expensive tea sets. By about 1810 handles were fitted to the bowl to form the now familiar teacup, and this form became almost universal. Legend says the handle was introduced and popularized by Madame de Pompadour.

COFFEE CANS AND CUPS

Coffee in England and on the Continent was often served in a can — a straight-sided cylinder with a handle jutting out at the right. It measured 2½" high and 2½" in diameter. The saucers were indented and called stands. Such coffee cans became fashionable in the second half of the eighteenth century up to 1820. After that time, the coffee can gave way to the more fanciful form of the coffee cup.

A coffee cup is normally tall and narrow in comparison to a teacup and has one handle. Although called coffee cups, they could be used for tea as well.

DEMITASSE CUPS

The demitasse cup originated in France and means "half a cup." These smaller coffee cups were first used to drink the stronger expresso coffee after a meal.

Espresso coffee originated in 1822 with the invention of the first crude expresso machine in France. The Italians perfected this machine and were the first to manufacture it. Espresso has become such an integral part of Italian life and culture that there are presently over 200,000 expresso bars in Italy.

SAUCERS

Saucers in their present form evolved out of the Oriental saucer-dish, with its slightly upward curving sides, central depression, and teacup stand, originally a simple circular stand with an indentation in the center to hold the cup steady. With its high sides, the saucer-dish was often regarded as no more than a shallow tea bowl, whose greater surface area allowed more rapid cooling of the liquid; thus, the early custom of drinking tea from the saucer rather than the cup. As teacups became larger, the saucers gradually shrunk in size.

TRIOS

A typical tea and coffee service in the eighteenth century consisted of 12 teacups or tea bowls, 12 coffee cans or cups, and 12 saucers. The saucer was used interchangeably with the can, cup, or bowl, as coffee and tea were rarely ever served at the same time. Today a tea bowl/cup, coffee can/cup, and saucer is referred to as a "trio" and is highly prized by English collectors. In his book *Guide to Understanding 19th and 20th Century British Porcelain*, David Battie says that apart from major pieces, "the most favored combination is the trio: teacup, coffee can, and saucer. Teacups must have saucers; coffee cans are still salable without them." Some American collectors use the term "trio" to refer to a cup, saucer, and dessert plate.

CHOCOLATE CUPS

Hot chocolate was a very popular drink in the eighteenth century, particularly in France, and many cups had a dual function. By the 1760s chocolate cups tended to be larger and taller than coffee cups, sometimes with two handles and a cover.

CUP PLATES

In days when handleless tea bowls were used, it was fashionable and more practical to pour the hot liquid into the deep saucer and drink from it. While this polite saucer sipping was going on, the cup was rested in a special cup plate, a little flat dish about three or four inches in diameter. The first cup plates were made of earthenware pottery. In the United States glass cup plates were often favored. By 1840, cup plates were no longer in style.

BREAKFAST CUPS

These large cups held two regular sized cups of coffee or tea and were often included in a full tea service.

"One should drink out of a good breakfast cup — that is, the cylindrical-type of cup, not the flat, shallow type. The breakfast cup holds more, and with the other kind, one's tea is always half cold before one has started on it." (George Orwell, "A Nice Cup of Tea," *Evening Standard*, 1/12/46.)

SHAPES AND HANDLES

1750 – 1800

Early shapes were often quite plain with simple lines. Many cups were molded into lovely floral or fruit forms. Vertical fluting became popular, and Meissen's Royal Flute shape was introduced in 1775. Coffee cups were straight-sided, and the bucket-shaped can was developed in 1790. Early tea bowls had straight foot rims. Loop handles were common, some with inner spurs, others with Chinese-style flattened thumb rests. In France, curved ear-shaped handles were popular on Old Paris cups. Sevres coffee cans had the much copied kicked loop handle.

1800 – 1815

By 1800, the dominant shape was the Royal Flute, scalloped and waisted with a kicked loop handle. The plain, rounded Bute shape was introduced with a plain loop or ring handle. The squat, slightly flared, rimmed Porriger shape was popular in England. The square French handle was developed in 1800. The lemon-shaped cup with pulled-up handle was developed in Berlin about 1800 and was called the Campaner shape. Tea bowls had more rounded foot rims. The Empire and Fragonard shapes were developed in France.

1815 – 1845

By the 1820s, the influence of the Romantic Movement began to affect all aspects of interior design. The ladies who swooned over Lord Byron's poems wanted more flamboyant tea wares. The dominant cup shape, the London shape, was introduced in 1812, and it remained popular until 1830. Fluted cups of many styles with coiled, French loop, old English, and "D" shaped handles were in vogue. The Adelaide shape was introduced in 1835 and the footed Glasgow shape in 1845. Gadrooning, often used in silver designs, was popular. This decorative series of curved, inverted flutings, somewhat like a clenched fist, was used on a variety of shapes.

1845 – 1875

Waisted cups with divided handles, sometimes with leaf terminals, were fashionable. Deep footed or pedestal cups were popular. Straight-lined and tapered cups were evident. Oval ring, loop, and rope handles were in style.

1875 – Present

This period saw the beginnings of the Art Nouveau movement that spread across the United States, England, and the Continent. The movement was characterized by flowing, sensuous lines, swirling leaf and floral forms, and other naturalistic motifs. Cups were made in the shapes of molded flowers and leaves, often with twig handles and feet or shaped like coral branches.

In 1896 Joseph Shelley introduced his famous Dainty White six-flute shape, and the next 50 years produced other delicate, fluted shapes. The Art Deco movement of the 1920s and 1930s produced angular shapes and handles, such as the Vogue and Mode shapes.

Although a large factory might have produced hundreds of new patterns each year, shapes are used repeatedly because of the enormous expense of introducing a new shape. For this reason, manufacturers put names or numbers on their shapes.

Illustrations by Charlene Margiotta

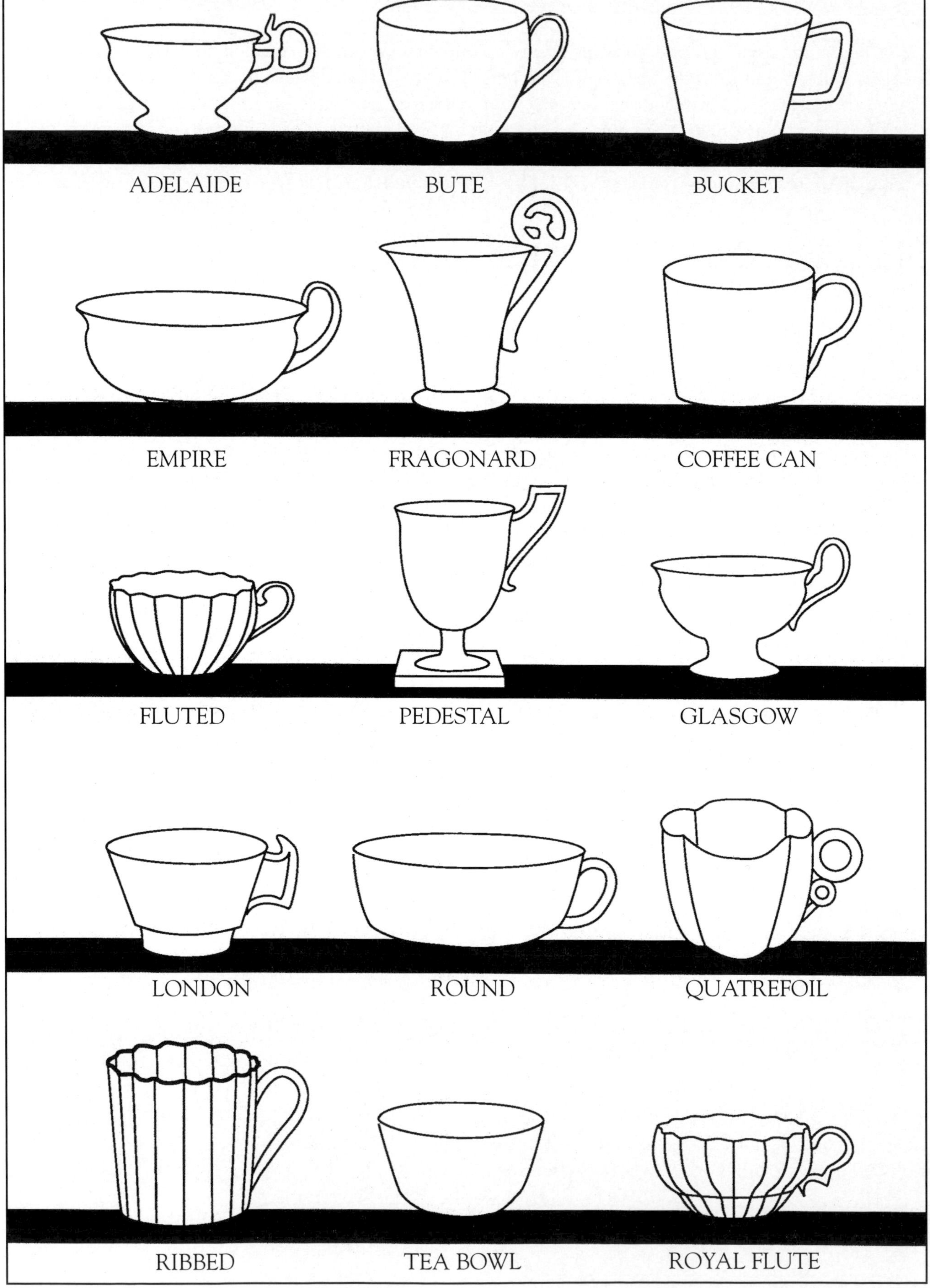

ADELAIDE

BUTE

BUCKET

EMPIRE

FRAGONARD

COFFEE CAN

FLUTED

PEDESTAL

GLASGOW

LONDON

ROUND

QUATREFOIL

RIBBED

TEA BOWL

ROYAL FLUTE

Illustrations by Charlene Margiotta

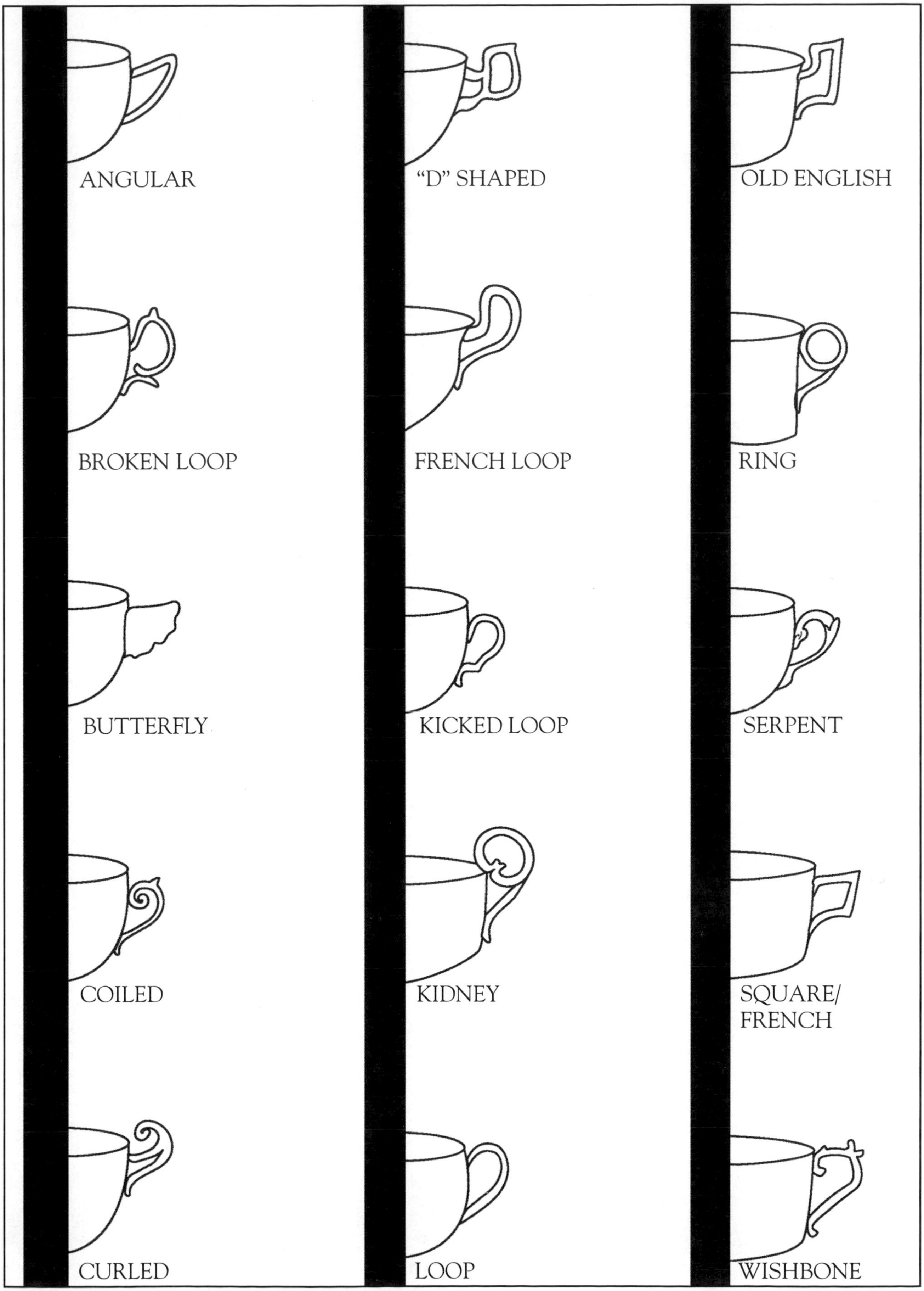

ANGULAR

"D" SHAPED

OLD ENGLISH

BROKEN LOOP

FRENCH LOOP

RING

BUTTERFLY

KICKED LOOP

SERPENT

COILED

KIDNEY

SQUARE/ FRENCH

CURLED

LOOP

WISHBONE

THE MANUFACTURING PROCESS

A DEFINITION OF PORCELAIN

Porcelain is the name originally given to the Chinese ware brought to Europe by the Portuguese and Italian traders returning home with treasures from the Far East. For centuries porcelain was a secret known only to the Chinese. When Marco Polo, the Venetian explorer, returned home from the court of Kublai Khan in the thirteenth century, he named the rare pieces of china he brought home with him "porcelana" because the glassy surface and texture reminded him of a seashell he knew, a cowrie called porcelli in Italian.

THE INGREDIENTS

There are two kinds of porcelain: soft-paste and hard-paste. Soft-paste porcelain differs from hard or true porcelain in that it contains large amounts of ground glass which enable it to be fired at much lower temperatures. Soft-paste porcelain is vitreous and translucent.

True, or hard-paste, porcelain is composed principally of feldspar, quartz, and kaolin, which produce a fine clay that is virtually free of impurities. The relative amounts of these three ingredients vary according to the texture that is desired. The more kaolin, the harder the porcelain. Fired at very high temperatures, hard-paste porcelain is characteristically translucent and white, and has great strength and hardness. It is almost always cast in molds. The beauty and decorative potential of the pure white clay more than compensates for the technical problems involved in its production. As the process and materials for hard-paste porcelain became better understood, the making of soft-paste porcelain was gradually phased out for tea ware.

The ingredients of porcelain are carefully washed, ground, and pulverized before they are mixed together. Water is then pressed out of the creamy liquid, and this results in a workable clay which can be stored until it is needed.

PREPARATION

There are two basic methods of taking a shapeless lump of clay and making it into an object of beauty and usefulness like a cup or saucer. Throwing is one method, and molding is another. The throwing method is certainly not for mass producing an item, but it has a kind of charm. In the throwing method, a portion of clay is centered on the potter's wheel, and as it rotates, the potter skillfully shapes it with his hands to the desired form. It has that one-of-a-kind personal touch that is not possible in mass production.

Molding is ideal for long production runs of objects which have to be identical in form and size and for intricate shapes. When cakes of clay paste are obtained in a workable state, they are ready for one of three methods of molding: jiggering, jollying, or casting.

After any one of the three processes is completed, the piece is trimmed and sponged to a smooth finish. If assembly of the pieces is required, for instance a handle to a cup, this is accomplished by using slip to attach it to the cup form.

DESIGNING AND MODELING

To create a new shape, a designer must first draw each item and establish a design. A mold must then be made before a piece of fine porcelain can be produced. The modeller must bear in mind that there will be a reduction in size during the bisque firing, so the model must be at least six percent larger than the finished item. The mold is usually made of plaster of Paris or a resin material.

Cups and saucers are actually produced from working molds. These molds are exact copies in the reverse of the original models. Molds must be very dry before they are used, so that the dry plaster wall will quickly absorb moisture from the paste. To produce a single item in large quantities, many working molds may be required as the molds wear out. In a cup and saucer, a working mold is required for the shape of the cup itself, another mold for the handle, and one for the saucer. Slip is used for the adhesive. Making these separate working molds is a true art requiring great skill. Model and mold making is one of the most important parts of the production process. (See photos on page 21.)

Photos on this page courtesy of Pickard, Inc., Antioch, Illinois.

Molding

Attaching the foot

Finishing application of foot

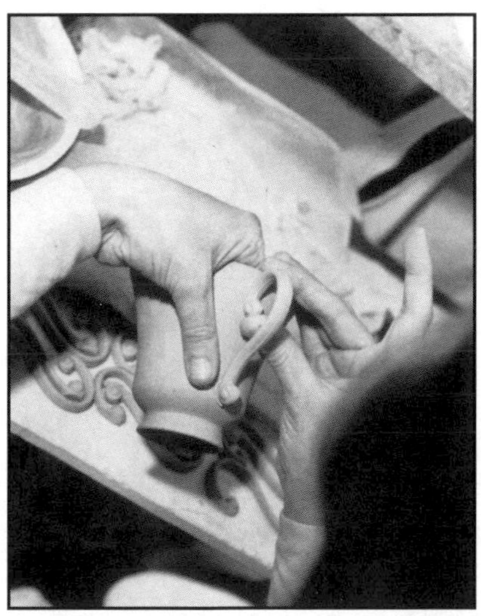

Attaching handle

Putting cups in racks for firing in kiln

Lining cup

Applying decal to saucer

BISQUE FIRING

The first firing of a piece is called bisque or biscuit and requires very careful handling. The molded piece goes into a kiln. It takes a piece about 30 hours of firing, and the piece will reach temperatures as high as 1750° F. After cooling to room temperature, it is ready for further processing. (See photo on page 21.)

GLAZE

The glaze applied to a cup and saucer serves several purposes. The first is to form a completely impenetrable surface; secondly, to provide durability to the items for long and hard usage; and lastly, to produce the translucency which is characteristic of a fine porcelain cup and saucer.

Quartz, feldspar, chalk, and dolomite are mixed together to make a creamy liquid called glaze. The ingredients may vary slightly from company to company for the desired effect.

Glaze is applied to a cup or saucer by dipping it in a vat of the liquid. The bisque piece is very absorbent, and a layer of glaze is built up. The glaze must be of just the right thickness.

LAST FIRING

After glazing, a cup is put in a kiln for a second firing, which is done at about 2100°F. More firings may be required depending on the quality and degree of painting and gilding desired.

FINAL TOUCHES

After the final firing, some cups and saucers may be lined. Lining is accomplished when a cup is placed on a spinning platform, and an artist applies a brush to the rim of the cup and/or saucer. This is usually gold, silver, or enamels. A decal can also be put in place at this time. (See photo on page 21.)

Porcelain may be decorated at a number of stages in its production. Prior to glazing, the bisque ware is often decorated with colored underglazes or stains. The glaze is applied to the bisque and fired at a much lower temperature than the clay body itself. After the ware has been glazed and fired, it is often further decorated with overglaze enamels, metallic lusters, or decals and then fired yet again at an even lower temperature.

The final step of the manufacturing process is the inspection. To be acceptable a cup and saucer must be free of any defects. Although there are inspections along the way, it's very important that a final inspection is completed. The cup is lightly tapped to determine if it is cracked. If the cup is not cracked, it produces a clear ringing sound. If it is cracked it makes a dull sound.

When all the processes have been completed, with some minor variations depending on the specific manufacturer, we have a beautiful finished cup and saucer ready for decoration. In November 1944 Syracuse China published a newsletter stating that cups were produced by crews of 12 people working together. The crew consisted of a lining maker, a lining "snatcher," a cup maker, a mold runner, a cup remover, two cup turners, a cup sponger, two handlers, and two handle makers.

DECORATIVE TECHNIQUES

MOLDED DESIGNS

The early forms of decoration were often molded designs or intricate relief decoration like the ones achieved by the Meissen Company in their famous Swan Service. Sprig-molded ornamentation derived from Chinese porcelain occurred on early English porcelain as well.

MONOCHROME/POLYCHROME ENAMELS

Painting in a single color such as black, brown, blue, sepia, and gold, or different shades of these colors, is called monochrome painting. This form was largely used in France and Germany during the eighteenth century.

Polychrome enameling is the use of two or more colors. Johann Höroldt, manager of the Meissen Company in the 1720s, developed 16 enamel paints which are still the basic paints for porcelain decoration today. His contributions made Meissen a leader in polychrome enamel painting, and his unique style is still being used. In contrast to the blue and white ware, the shapes of early polychrome enameled porcelain tea bowls and saucers are much simpler, relying entirely on the effect of the pale, glowing colors of the enamels, highlighted by gilding.

HAND PAINTING

A skilled porcelain artist paints a picture on a cup and saucer in the same manner that any artist would paint a picture on a canvas. The picture could be a portrait, landscape, animals, flowers, or designs. Hand painting was the favored method of decoration on the elegant tea ware commissioned by the wealthy and titled classes. Tiny sprigs of flowers, swags of leaves and garlands of rose buds, and exotic birds were some of the lovely designs on porcelain cups and saucers of the eighteenth century. Toward the end of the eighteenth century a new fashion in decoration was introduced to the world of elegant tea ware for which Derby porcelain was largely responsible. Scenic and landscape painting of a very high quality was produced, and an amazing "wash" effect similar to a watercolor painting was created.

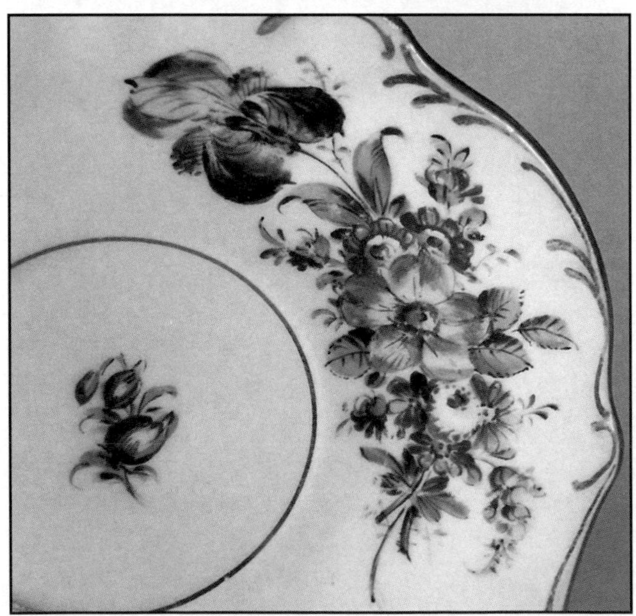

PORTRAIT PAINTING

Portrait painting was often used as a method of decorating a cabinet cup and saucer. The face of a beautiful woman was a common subject, although famous men were often used as well. Full human forms were also popular, and many cups and saucers can be found with both men and women together, often in the form of lovers posed in a garden. This type of decoration was very expensive to produce and is not found on ordinary tea or coffee services.

GILDING

Gold ornamentation has been used to enhance fine porcelains since the early Oriental tea wares were imported into England and the Continent in the seventeenth century. Early methods were japanned, oil, and honey gilding.

Acid gilding was introduced at Minton in 1865 and was later used by most of the leading producers of porcelain cups and saucers. The pleasing contrast between matte and shiny gold is achieved by the use of acid. The parts to be left matte are recessed by acid so that when the gold is applied, the raised surface only is burnished, leaving the gold dull and matte where the design had been etched into the surface of the cup and saucer.

Regardless of the method used, collectors treasure cups and saucers that are decorated with gilding. Cups that are gilded on the inside were not usually used for drinking but for display.

BEADING

Beading is a decorative method of using beads of clay. These beads may be either cast, applied, or embossed. The effect is obtained by applying beads or dots of slip to achieve the desired effect. The beads are fired and then

enameled or gilded. Beading is found mostly as a trim decoration.

JEWELING

"Jewels" are made by dabbing dots of different colored enameling, richly colored glaze, or gilt on the cup and saucer to simulate jewels, such as turquoise, rubies, or pearls. Examples of

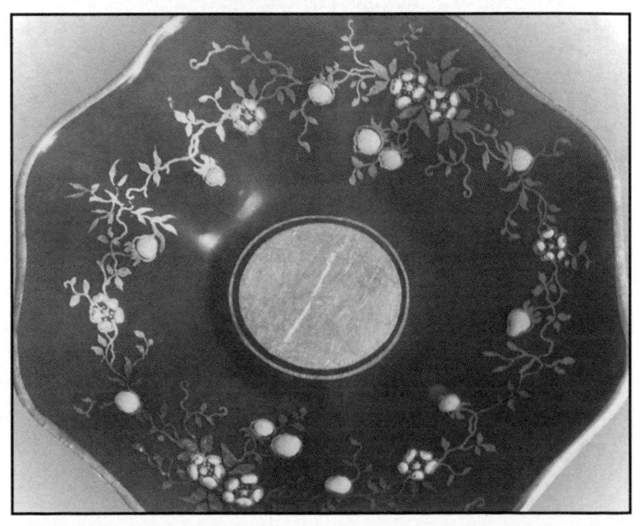

jeweled cups and saucers are highly regarded by collectors today.

LACE

A lace effect on porcelain is achieved by simply using a piece of real lace and dipping it in porcelain or gilt slip. After this is accomplished and the lace is saturated, it is applied to the cup and saucer and then it is placed in a kiln and fired, at which time the lace is burned away, leaving a porcelain imprint of the lace. This process was first used at Meissen about 1770.

TRANSFER PRINTING

Transfer printing was introduced in the 1750s to achieve a high level of detail and accuracy as well as to produce a high volume of items with identical patterns at a relatively low cost. This process was well suited for cups and saucers.

Transfer printing involved putting a design on paper then transferring it to a copper plate. This was accomplished by piercing the paper with small holes to outline the details of the pattern. The paper was then laid on a copper plate and a fine powder was sprinkled on the surface to make an image. This image was then engraved into the plate by a sharp instrument. Once an item was engraved, hundreds of articles could be decorated with the same design. Semi-skilled painters could fill in the outline at a fraction of the cost of skilled painters.

Around 1800 another method of engraving, called bat printing, was introduced. The design was transferred from the copper plate to a glazed cup and saucer by a bat of glue and another substance. The copper plate was charged with an oily substance, the gluey bat was transferred to the article, and powdered color was then dusted over the article to adhere to the oiled parts.

DECAL DECORATION

The decal method of decorating a cup and saucer is the process of transferring a design or picture from specially prepared paper sheets, which are printed lithographically.

When the paper is put in water, the decal will slide off and adhere to a cup and saucer. This process is done before putting the objects in the kiln. The decal can be left as it is or in some cases enhanced by additional painting. A decal printed cup and saucer is easily detected by using a magnifying glass or a jeweler's loupe. If you can see dots, it's a decal.

SILVER OVERLAY

This form of decorating a cup and saucer during the late nineteenth and early twentieth century was very popular. Silver overlay is a decoration or network of silver, usually sterling, which is applied to a cup and saucer by a silver craftsman after the pieces are completely finished. Many silver manufacturers were involved in this kind of decoration. Silver overlay can be engraved with floral, fruit, and rococo swirls. It is often difficult to find a maker's mark on the silver overlay.

SILVER DEPOSIT

Porcelain manufacturers used silver makers for electro-depositing sterling silver patterns on their cups and saucers as well as other items. A liquid silver can also be painted on with a brush. Silver deposit is very thin and not raised as with silver overlay. It is much cheaper to produce than sterling silver overlay.

EARLY MANUFACTURERS

CHINESE EXPORT

The lovely tea ware brought over from China by the East India Company to Europe, England, and America was immediately successful. Porcelain manufacturing in China was at Ching-tê-chên, where the population was more than one million, and 3,000 kilns were in operation during the eighteenth century. Much of the porcelain was sent as blanks to Canton, where it was big business to decorate porcelain tea ware for export to Europe and America.

Chinese export tea ware had three major designs in the early eighteenth century: Oriental motifs, such as the Blue Willow pattern (chinoiserie); designs adapted from European prints; and armorials, which were coats-of-arms of important European and American families.

JAPANESE IMARI

Imari porcelain was manufactured in Japan as early as the seventeenth century, and it was named after the harbor town of Imari from which it was exported to Europe. Imari is easily recognized by the rich iron-red and luminous blue colors, often enhanced with gilt. A characteristic design is bamboo and cherry blossoms or brushwood hedges growing out of stylized rocks. Japanese Imari was imitated by the Meissen Company and many of the English porcelain factories.

MEISSEN COMPANY

The first European porcelain company was founded in Meissen, Germany, in 1710 and was called the Royal Saxon Porcelain Manufactory. Although the Chinese had been using hard-paste porcelain for a long time, the development of porcelain in Europe was the result of a collaboration of three people: physicist Walther von Tschirnausen, alchemist Johann Frederick Böttger, and their patron, Augustus the Strong, Elector of Saxony.

One of the earliest hand-painted examples of porcelain made by Böttger at Meissen was a cup and saucer. The cup was made before 1714 and had an enameled coat-of-arms of Sophia, Electress of Hanover, who died in 1714. A flowering tree was on the reverse of the cup.

During the mid-eighteenth century, Oriental scenes were favored by the court, and tea ware was created with the well known chinoiserie designs, as well as the Japanese dragon patterns. Early tea bowls can be found in these styles, often with gilt scrollwork and foot rims.

VIENNA

The second European porcelain factory was founded in Vienna, Austria, by Claudius I. DuPaquier in 1718. The factory was soon producing tea ware of good glaze and admirable quality.

HAUSMALERS

From the seventeenth century in Germany and Austria there was an important industry of free-lance artists who decorated faience to help factories meet the demand for highly decorated pottery. These decorators worked in their own studios or at home. Once porcelain was discovered in Europe, these hausmalers obtained blanks from Meissen or Vienna and painted for resale.

SEVRES

Sevres is the luxury name in French porcelain. The earliest product, a soft-paste porcelain which was translucent and flawless, was first made in 1745 at Vincennes under the blessings of Louis XV. By the early 1800s only hard-paste porcelains were being made.

EUROPEAN DECORATIVE STYLES

The styles of early cup and saucer modeling and decorating were influenced by the artistic and architectural styles of the day.

1710 – 1740 BAROQUE STYLE

The Baroque style is characterized by massive form and vigorous movement. Heavily ornamented tableware was enriched with vivid ground colors.

1735 – 1775 ROCOCO STYLE

French in origin, this style is characterized by light graceful designs and fanciful forms. Cup handles have curves and scrolls. Fruits and flowers are strewn all over in a light and delicate manner.

1800 – 1820 EMPIRE STYLE

This French neoclassical style originated during the reign of Napoleon and is characterized by straight lines and symmetry. Influenced by archaeological discoveries in Pompeii in the 1770s, the decoration of the ancient Greeks and Romans became fashionable.

1820 – 1845 BIEDERMEIER

This is the German continuation of the Empire style. Decorations and forms typified the simple tastes of the middle class *bourgeois* and is identical to England's early Victorian style.

THE ENGLISH POTTERS

When the Grand Union Canal was completed in Great Britain in 1772, the cost of transport fell dramatically. It became possible for thousands of ordinary households in England to replace their pewter and silver cups and horn mugs with china tableware. The growth in popularity of tea drinking created an entirely new business for the pottery industry at Stoke-on-Trent in Staffordshire and throughout England.

Three major technical innovations influenced the manufacture of china tableware and its accessibility to a wider audience.

WEDGWOOD'S CREAMWARE

In 1760 Josiah Wedgwood produced the first commercially successful earthenware which was pale enough to resemble porcelain. It was named creamware and has been called Britain's great contribution in the history of ceramics. It could be painted or printed like porcelain, usually after glazing. Queen Charlotte was so pleased with the ware she allowed it to be called Queen's ware.

Perhaps the most famous dinner service in the world was the 952-piece creamware set produced by Wedgwood for the Empress Catherine of Russia in 1773 – 74. It was decorated with 1,244 views of scenic Great Britain.

SPODE'S DISCOVERY OF BONE CHINA

Josiah Spode II (1754 – 1827) is credited with the discovery of bone china. Bone ash is combined with china clay, thus giving it more stability. By 1800 other factories were adding bone ash to china clay as well. This became the standard English porcelain body throughout the nineteenth century and remains popular today. The light weight and translucency of bone china makes it appealing for tea ware. It has been said that if you hold a teacup up to the light and can see the shadow from your hand through it, it is bone china.

TRANSFER DECORATION

Transfer printing was introduced in the 1750s to achieve a high level of detail and accuracy as well as to produce a high volume of items with identical patterns at a relatively low cost. As a result of this technology, hundreds of factories began operating in the Staffordshire district of England.

English Staffordshire cups and saucers can be found in the usual colors produced by transfer printing — black, light blue, dark blue, pink, brown, sepia, green, and mulberry. Scenic castles and towers were favorite designs of early English potters. Pastoral scenes, Continental views, landscapes, Chinese motifs, and colorful fruit and flower patterns, as well as various sprig designs, can be found. Some cups and saucers may have a brown or black floral transfer pattern, with flowers and leaves colored by hand. Most pot-

teries maintained a group of young girls to do this coloring.

MINTON

In 1793 Thomas Minton, with two other partners, opened a pottery in Stoke-on-Trent. For the first few years blue-printed earthenwares were made similar to those made by other companies in the area. In 1798 cream-colored earthenware and bone china were introduced, greatly increasing the sales of the company. During this early period, production was concentrated on table, tea, and dessert wares. Surviving pattern books show a great variety of printed, enamel painted, and gilded designs. Subjects were landscapes, chinoiseries, French-inspired floral patterns, lusters, and neoclassical designs.

MASON, CHARLES JAMES & CO.

The Mason Brothers, who operated one of the most successful nineteenth century Staffordshire pottery companies, began to produce a brightly colored, extremely durable range of tea wares in a heavy, faintly transparent earthenware with a metallic ring. They patented it in 1813 as Ironstone China, and it was instantly successful. Patterns were based on the richly gilded, bright colored Japanese designs popular at the time.

OTHER EARLY MANUFACTURERS

Davenport (1794 – 1887) was primarily an earthenware manufacturer but made bone china tea ware after 1810. Early pieces were seldom marked and can be identified by pattern numbers. Ridgway began operation in 1792 and produced a vast amount of tea ware in brightly colored grounds. Although few Ridgway porcelains have a factory mark, most have pattern numbers. A few other early ceramic manufacturers that produced fine quality tea ware are William Adams & Sons, Samuel Alcock & Co., Copeland & Garrett, H. & R. Daniel, and New Hall.

Many early English teacups and coffee cans are unmarked, and it is a challenging task for the collector to identify the maker. This can sometimes be accomplished by researching pattern numbers and date marks, or becoming familiar with a particular factory.

THE UNITED STATES

In the eighteenth century it was almost impossible to find American china fine enough to decorate the home. Although potteries had sprung up all over the United States, they produced utilitarian wares such as redware, stoneware and yellow ware almost exclusively. Buyers looked to China and Europe for their fine porcelain.

William Ellis Tucker opened a porcelain factory in Philadelphia in 1826. At first, decorative and useful Queen's ware was made in the classical shapes of the Empire style. Many designs were copied from English and French porcelains. Tucker was the first company to use American subject matter on porcelain, and his designs included historical views and patriotic heroes. Many pieces were unmarked to resemble unmarked French porcelains.

Coffee cup and saucer.

Unidentified underglaze blue mark, nineteenth century, probably German.

Octagonal shape with unusual twisted handle; pink luster with geometric and gold bands.

$70.00 – 90.00.

Breakfast cup and saucer.

Societe de Faiencerie de Salens, c. 1868 – 1880.

Large round majolica cup with loop handle; colorful relief molded fruit. (See mark #113.)

$100.00 – 125.00.

Demitasse cup and saucer.

Sevres, 1846.

Can with loop handle, deep saucer; pale blue with gilt decoration.

$125.00 – 150.00.

Teacup and saucer.

Choisy-le-Roi, c. 1870s.

Octagon-shaped majolica cup and saucer, square handle; relief geometric decoration.

$100.00 – 125.00.

Demitasse cup and saucer.

Chinese Rose Canton, c. 1870s.

Tapered cup with foot ring, unusual handle; band of magnificent enameled butterflies, hand-painted birds, flowers, and orange-red butterflies outlined in gold in lower band of cup and center of saucer.

$175.00 – 200.00.

Tea bowl and saucer.

William Adams & Sons Ltd., c. 1819 – 1864.

Ironstone paneled bowl; Oriental black and white transfer.

$75.00 – 100.00.

Tea bowl and saucer.

William Adams & Sons Ltd. (elaborate Britannia backstamp with pattern name and "stone china"), c. 1825 – 1850.

Twelve-sided bowl and saucer, Gothic paneled shape; Isola Bella pattern on stone china (ironstone wares).

$80.00 – 120.00.

Coffee cup and saucer.

Alcock, Samuel, c. 1840s.

Lobed cup with wishbone handle; beautifully gilt and decorated with cobalt blue oak leaves and sprays of pink roses and purple thistles.

$100.00 – 125.00.

Coffee can and saucer.

Bodley, E. J. D., c. 1875+.

Bucket-shaped can with loop handle; hand-painted daisies on pink ground.

$100.00 – 125.00.

Coffee cup and saucer.

Unmarked attributed to Bodley, Pattern #3770, English Registry mark, c. 1875.

Six-paneled cup and saucer with molded square bamboo handle; landscape scenes in enameled colors.

$75.00 – 95.00.

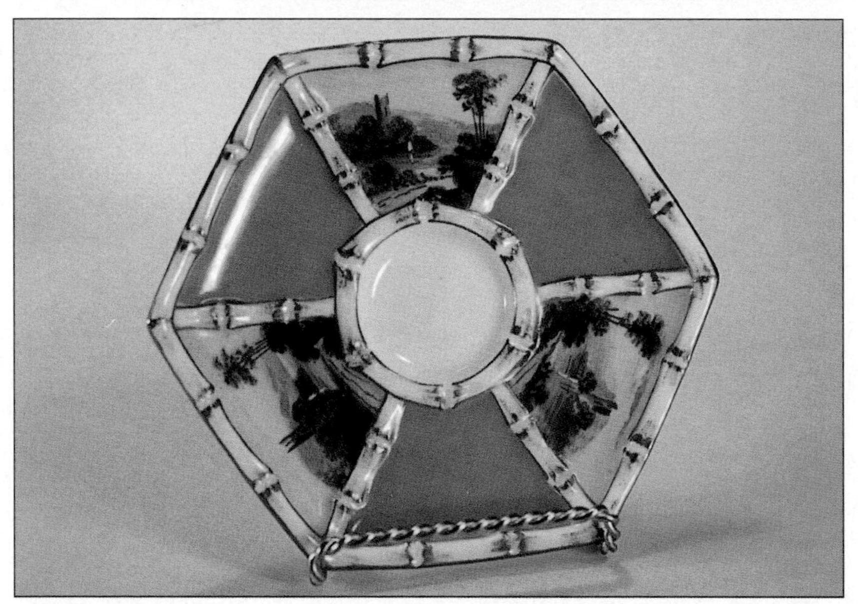

Another view of above saucer.

Teacup and saucer (miniature).

Caughley, c. 1775 – 1799.

Straight-sided footed cup with fat loop handle; blue and white chinoiserie.

$400.00 – 450.00.

Coffee can.

Caughley, c. 1780.

Slightly tapered can with flared lip, grooved loop handle; Three Flowers pattern printed in underglaze blue.

$230.00 – 275.00.

Tea bowl and saucer.

S. E. & C. Challinor, Fenton, c. 1860 – 1890.

Pearlware cup and saucer; carmine stylized flowers with black stems and green leaves.

$75.00 – 95.00.

Teacup, coffee cup, and saucer trio.

Copeland & Garrett, c. 1833 – 1847.

Footed, scalloped cups with fancy handles; gilt decoration on white.

$250.00 – 275.00.

Coffee cup and saucer.

Coalport, c. 1825 – 1830.

Fluted cup with "Old English" handle; hand-painted, enameled flowers on white reserves, elaborately gilded on a dark blue ground.

$200.00 – 225.00.

Coffee cup and saucer.

Coalport, c. 1835.

Straight-sided cup with loop handle; net embossed design decorated with a hand-painted pattern of blue and yellow spots with enameled flowers within a pink and gilt edged cartouche.

$250.00 – 275.00.

Teacup and saucer.

Daniel, H. & R., c. 1830.

Rare molded cup in "Mayflower" shape; hand-painted decoration of enameled flowers within a molded cartouche and surrounded by raised florets picked out in pale green, #4631.

$175.00 – 195.00.

Coffee can.

Derby, Bloor Period, c. 1820 – 1840.

Can with loop handle with inner and outer spurs; four panels outside and six panels on inside rim; Imari variation in cobalt blue, orange, red, and green enamels with gilt.

$200.00 – 225.00.

Coffee can and saucer.

Hobson, G. & J., Burslem, England, c. 1875.

Bucket-shaped can with magnificent crane handle; hand-painted plants and flowers.

$150.00 – 175.00.

Teacup and saucer.

Unmarked except for #6286, attributed to Minton, c. 1850s.

Straight-sided cup with ring handle; lovely gold star design with roses, turquoise band, gilt.

$100.00 – 125.00.

Teacup and saucer.

Minton, pseudo Sevres mark, early nineteenth century.

Bute-shaped cup with ring handle; lovely hand-painted flowers with dark blue underglaze peacock.

$400.00 – 450.00.

Coffee can.

Minton, c. 1811.

Can with ring handle; red flowers with gilt leaves in band on upper portion.

$150.00 – 175.00.

Coffee can.

Minton, c. 1809.

Can with ring handle; gilt "seaweed" type scrolling in band on upper half.

$125.00 – 150.00.

Coffee can.

Pattern #104 in green, attributed to Minton, c. 1801.

Can with ring handle; multicolor enamels and gilded rim and handle; chinoiserie square "rocks," flowers, vines, and orange bugs; floral sprigs on reverse.

$150.00 – 190.00.

Teacup and saucer.

Francis Morley & Co., Shelton, Hanley, c. 1850.

Twelve-sided cup, 16-sided saucer on ironstone body, unusual loop and spur handle; Vista pattern.

$80.00 – 100.00.

Teacup and saucer.

New Hall Porcelain Works, c. 1812 – 1835.

London-style cup, deep saucer; Oriental scene with gilt decoration.

$100.00 – 125.00.

Coffee can.

Unmarked, attributed to New Hall, c. 1805.

Can with ring handle; multicolor enamels and gilded; chinoiserie type building with beehive and orange tree on reverse.

$180.00 – 220.00.

Coffee cup and saucer.

Ridgway, c. 1825.

Gadroon-edge footed cup with high loop handle; cobalt blue inside cup with hand-painted flowers, simple gilt decoration.

$100.00 – 125.00.

Tea bowl and saucer.

Ridgway, c. 1830 – 1840.

Tricolor bowl and saucer.

$200.00 – 250.00.

Coffee can and saucer.

Ridgway, c. 1870.

Can with square handle; Devonshire pattern.

$175.00 – 225.00.

Teacup and saucer.

Spode, #7779, c. 1815 – 1825.

London shape cup and deep saucer; cobalt blue leaf and acorn pattern around cup and saucer; slightly faded gilt on saucer.

$100.00 – 125.00.

Teacup and saucer.

Spode, c. 1815 – 1825.

London shape cup; chinoiserie polychrome decoration.

$250.00 – 300.00.

Teacup and saucer.

Spode, c. 1826.

Footed cup, shaped and gadrooned rims, kidney handle; richly decorated in the Frog pattern, #4233.

$125.00 – 150.00.

Coffee can and saucer.

Wedgwood, c. 1780 – 1820.

Basalt can with loop handle, deep saucer; molded puttis.

$400.00 – 450.00.

Coffee can and saucer.

Wedgwood jasper ware; c. 1860.

Can with broken loop handle; dancing muses.

$800.00 – 900.00.

Tea bowl, coffee cup, and saucer trio.

Worcester, eighteenth century.

Scalloped and swirled, loop handle with inner spur; cobalt and gilt border, scattered flowers.

$475.00 – 525.00.

Coffee can.

Worcester, Flight & Barr, c. 1792 – 1803.

Can with ring handle; acanthus leaf stylized scrolling, brown-carmine design with gilt leaves.

$175.00 – 200.00.

Coffee can.

Worcester, Barr, Flight, Barr, c. 1807 – 1813.

Can with ring handle; red and brown stylized flowers with red branches and gilt leaves.

$170.00 – 190.00.

Coffee can and saucer.

Royal Worcester, c. 1875.

Bucket-shaped can with decorated loop handle, deep saucer; leafy transfer. (See mark #119.)

$100.00 – 125.00.

Teacup and saucer.

Yates, c. 1825.

Fluted cup with "Old English" handle; hand-painted enameled flowers within a gilt cartouche on a pink ground, pattern #1037.

$100.00 – 125.00.

Teacup and saucer.

Unmarked, probably English, late nineteenth century.

Heavy stoneware, 12-panelled molded cup and saucer, broken loop handle; molded flow blue design.

$40.00 – 50.00.

Teacup and saucer.

English, registry mark, c. 1871.

Majolica bucket-shaped tree bark cup with twisted twig handle; cherry blossoms on white.

$250.00 – 300.00.

Tea bowl and saucer.

Unmarked, c. 1830.

London-shaped bowl without handle, deep saucer; hand-painted sprig ware.

$50.00 – 75.00.

Teacup and saucer.

Unmarked except red triangle, c. 1800 – 1815.

Bute-shaped cup with reinforced loop handle; stylized "Japan" floral design in Imari colors dominated by large blue enameled leaves with gilt overlay.

$150.00 – 175.00.

Teacup and saucer.

Unmarked, c. 1825 – 1835.

Footed and out-flared cup with Old English stepped handle; green transfer print of lady and landscape.

$50.00 – 75.00.

Tea bowl and saucer.

Unmarked, Staffordshire, c. 1830 – 1840.

Footed bowl; pink transfer of pastoral scene.

$100.00 – 150.00.

Tea bowl and saucer.

Unmarked, Staffordshire, possibly Heath, c. 1820 – 1830.

Scalloped bowl and deep saucer; blue and white transfer of church and boy fishing.

$200.00 – 225.00.

Tea bowl and saucer.

Unmarked pearlware, c. 1820s.

Swirled and waisted; polychrome rose.

$140.00 – 160.00.

Teacup and saucer (miniature).

Staffordshire, nineteenth century.

Flared footed cup; Poonah pattern.

$150.00 – 175.00.

Coffee can.

Unmarked, unknown maker, c. 1808.

Can with kicked loop handle; unusual stylized "8" design with multicolor overenamels.

$130.00 – 160.00.

Teacup and saucer.

Unknown maker, three dots on cup, c. 1820 – 1830.

Bute-shaped bone china cup with ring handle and thumb rest; carmine red, bone, and pink.

$80.00 – 120.00.

Teacup and saucer.

Unknown maker, no marks, c. 1820 – 1830.

Bute-shaped bone china cup with loop handle and top thumb rest; hand-painted peach stylized flowers on silver luster.

$70.00 – 90.00.

Teacup and saucer.

Unknown maker, red "O" on cup, "OO" on saucer, c. 1825 – 1835.

London-style cup; chinoiserie design, black transfer design with overenamels, man and woman by gazebo.

$70.00 – 90.00.

Teacup and saucer.

Unknown maker, unmarked, c. 1839 – 1845.

Pedestal out-flaring cup with rustic "bean handle"; chinoiserie orange printed "slamat" design, over enamels in green, blue, and rose, pagoda, fence, and "amoeba" rocks.

$70.00 – 90.00.

Teacup and saucer.

Unknown maker, unmarked, c. 1830 – 1840.

Pedestal outflaring cup, high ring handle; green transfer of bird, butterflies, dragonfly, and floral swigs.

$50.00 – 75.00.

Teacup and saucer.

Unknown maker, unmarked, c. 1825 – 1840.

Flared and fluted cup with broken loop handle, inner spur and thumb rest; green transfer of seaweed and shells.

$50.00 – 75.00.

Teacup and saucer.

Unknown maker, unmarked, c. 1830 – 1840.

Fluted, ridged, and footed cup, broken loop handle; five raised geometric sprigs on cup and six on saucer covered with lilac enamel.

$50.00 – 70.00.

Teacup and saucer.

Unknown maker, unmarked, c. 1820 – 1835.

London-style cup; net embossed with over-enamel florals in cartouches, blue flowers separate cartouches, "ticked" floral circular design in center of saucer and interior cup ring.

$50.00 – 75.00.

Teacup and saucer.

Unknown maker, marked with two small circles, c. 1820 – 1835.

London-style cup; stylized florals and "ticked" design, "eyeball" roses along rim of cup and saucer and in cup interior and center of saucer.

$50.00 – 65.00.

Teacup and saucer.

Unknown maker, saucer marked 286 in pink at rim.

Fluted and ridged pedestal cup, unusual broken loop handle; multi-row clusters of blue and green enamel dots, faded luster trim.

$50.00 – 65.00.

Tea bowl and saucer.

Unknown maker, marked #1031 in pink below rim of saucer, c. 1820 – 1845.

Rose, red, and brown over-enamels, roses and yellow floral clusters alternate around cup and saucer.

$50.00 – 75.00.

Coffee cup, no saucer.

Unknown maker, c. 1840 – 1850.

Twelve-sided pearlware cup with heavy loop handle and spur; medium blue "romantic" transfer, floral, shield, and diaper interior border.

$40.00 – 50.00.

Tea bowl and saucer.

Unmarked, c. 1825 – 1850.

Twelve-sided bowl, 16-sided saucer in pearlware ironstone; pink "romantic" transfer, two men greeting a sitting woman on cup.

$80.00 – 120.00.

Punch cup.

Unknown maker, c. 1825 – 1850.

Pearlware, 12-paneled pedestal cup with high "Old English" handle; early Flow Blue continuous pattern transfer.

$150.00 – 250.00.

CABINET CUPS & SAUCERS

STYLES

Highly treasured by advanced collectors are the exquisite cabinet cups and saucers made by the leading porcelain factories in Europe in the eighteenth and nineteenth centuries. These lovely cups and saucers were considered works of art and were proudly displayed in the estates of the nobility. They were so fine and fragile that one cannot believe that they were made for use; hence the term cabinet cup.

Cabinet cups and saucers are found in a variety of styles, many having been introduced at Sevres and KPM in the early nineteenth century. In *An Illustrated Dictionary of Ceramics*, John Cushion describes the following styles:

Berlin cup – A tall coffee cup on three paw feet, having a handle rising above the rim.

Fontainbleau cup – A small goblet-shaped cup with a stemmed base.

Fragonard cup – A small, drum-shaped cup with a slightly flaring base and rim, having a tall curved handle rising above the rim.

St. Cloud cup – A small coffee cup with cylindrical upper part, then tapering toward the foot-ring, lower sides reeded.

Swan cup – Cup in the form of a swan, with the curved neck forming handle and accompanied by an oval saucer; interior of cup and saucer well often gilded.

Vincennes cup – Small square-shaped cylindrical coffee cup with no foot rim, angular loop handle.

DECORATION

The finest artists of the time decorated the elaborate cabinet cups and saucers. The decoration, often done in compartments of richly scrolled medallions, had scenes and figures, sometimes alternating with floral bouquets. For the collector, artist-signed pieces are more valuable. The subject matter also influences price. Portraits are most valuable, followed by landscapes, animals and birds, and finally fruits and flowers.

Watteau paintings were copied by porcelain painters at Meissen in the eighteenth century and by many Dresden studios in the nineteenth century. The French painter Antoine Watteau (1684 – 1721) created colorful figures and groups, usually in a pastoral setting.

Jeweled specimens are highly regarded by collectors today. The "jewels" were made by dabbing spots of different color enameling or richly colored glaze or gilt to simulate jewels. Sevres is credited with some of the finest jeweled cabinet cups and saucers. In the 1890s jeweled porcelain became a specialty at Coalport. Each piece was applied with even rows of finely graduated, tiny enamel drops in turquoise, coral, or white. In a 1996 Christie's auction a Coalport cabinet cup and saucer, c. 1895, with turquoise jewels on gold brought $1,000.00.

Japanism is a decorating style found on cabinet cups and saucers in the late nineteenth century. After a long period of self-imposed isolation, Japan began trade with the West in the mid-nineteenth century. The first big exhibition of Japanese art in London in 1862 caused a sensation. Leading French and English porcelain manufacturers were inspired by this new style of design. Cups and saucers were decorated with dragon handles and common Japanese motifs, such as clouds, waves, fish, birds, bamboo, cherry, and prunus blossoms. The subjects were usually done in pastel shades or heavy gilt enamelwork.

TREMBLEUSES

The trembleuse was first introduced at the French Factory of St. Cloud in the early eighteenth century. This two-handled cup had a distinctive type of large saucer with a pronounced ring or rail in the middle to hold the base of the cup securely. The French name implies that these saucers were made for those with trembling or shaky hands, such as invalids.

Examples may be found in which the center ring is elaborately pierced, so that any liquid spilled over the side can drain into the bottom of the saucer. Similar objects known as teacup stands were made in silver or Sheffield plate, the central ring often being detachable.

Sometimes a deep well was used instead of the vertical ring, especially at the Sevres, Chelsea, and Derby factories. Trembleuses were rare and choice in their time and are more so today.

CABARET SERVICES

Cabaret services, déjeuners, or tete-a-tete sets were popular in France during the third quarter of the eighteenth century. They consist of an often ornately-shaped tray, small teapot or coffee pot, milk or cream pot, a sugar, and two or more small cups and saucers. These lovely sets of matching porcelain were sometimes fitted into ornate boxes for use in traveling. Cabaret sets are little treasures because they are small and delicate and decorated in the richest styles.

SOLITAIRE SERVICE

A solitaire service is a cabaret service for one person, often in a fitted traveling case. Solitaire services were a Berlin specialty in the late eighteenth century.

MAKERS

SEVRES

Sevres is the luxury name in French porcelain. The earliest product, a soft-paste porcelain which was translucent and flawless, was first made in 1745 at Vincennes under the blessings of Louis XV. By the early 1800s only hard-paste porcelains were being made. The background colors were rich and exquisite. Blue de roi, bleu turquoise, and rose pompadour were the company's most famous ground colors. The finest artists of the time decorated the elaborate cabinet cups and saucers with portrait, landscape, and floral reserves surrounded by panels of exquisite gilding. In 1807 a set of 12 cups and saucers was a gift from Napoleon to Prince William of Prussia. The service was richly decorated with famous fables written by the French writer Jean de la Fontaine.

Many imitations of Sevres eighteenth century style cups and saucers were produced by French and other European manufacturers in the nineteenth century. After the French Revolution large numbers of blank Sevres ware were sold to decorators. Collectors today should be aware that Sevres imitations abound.

OLD PARIS

From 1770 to the mid-1800s many porcelain companies grew up in and around Paris. Richly decorated table services and cabinet ware were made. This porcelain is recognized by its extreme whiteness and rich gilding.

Strewn flower sprigs, especially the cornflower and graceful borders, were favorite motifs, as well as landscapes and medallions of Cupids. Cup shapes were usually classical in design with elegant decoration. The gilded swan cup was a popular form. Although some examples were marked, many were not.

VIENNA

The Vienna Porcelain Factory, founded in 1718 by Claudius Du Paquier, was second to Meissen in producing hard-paste porcelain. From 1747 to 1784 the company reached its peak of fame. The chief modeller, Johann Niedermeyer, introduced new background colors. A fine cobalt blue rivaled Sevres's bleu roi. Today this cobalt blue shade is still a favorite with collectors.

Richly ornamented cabinet ware was made in the neoclassical and Empire styles, often decorated with magnificent reproductions of paintings by famous artists such as Kauffman, Rubens, and Wagner, as well as beautiful floral and elaborate gilding.

A specialty of Vienna in the early nineteenth century was the use of gilt bands on a colored ground, usually on a can shape. These exquisite coffee cans would have been displayed rather than used.

KINGS PORCELAIN MANUFACTORY (KPM)

KPM was bought and controlled in 1763 by Frederick the Great, who ran the factory according to his own ideas. The company was noted for its beautifully modeled and decorated tea and dessert services. Cabaret and solitaire services were exquisitely decorated with Watteau paintings, battle scenes, landscapes, and florals. In the 1780s KPM produced monochrome scenic decorations — painting in a single color — or different shades of the same color.

NYMPHENBURG

The Nymphenburg factory, located near Munich, was founded in 1747 by the Bavarian Elector. As with many German companies, Meissen styles influenced the type of wares made. During the early years, table services and decorative pieces were painted in a rococo style featuring Watteau scenes, birds, fruits, and flowers. In 1795 the company created the "Perl" tea service for a member of the Bavarian royal family. A raised "string of pearls" jeweling surrounded the rim of each 12-sided cup and saucer, which was elaborately gilded and decorated with landscape scenes.

UNION PORCELAIN WORKS

The Union Porcelain Works of Greenport, New York, was established by German potters about 1854 and purchased later by C. H. L. Smith and Thomas C. Smith. Some say this was the first American factory to produce true hard-paste porcelain that could compare favorably with that made in France.

Cups and saucers were richly decorated with oval reserves of hand-painted birds, butterflies, and flowers with ornate embellishments and gilding. Pierced tea ware was made, copying the rice-grain decoration of the Chinese porcelains of the eighteenth century. A series of small perforations about the size and shape of a grain of rice was made, and then they were filled and covered by a clear glaze, resulting in a highly translucent effect.

The famous Liberty cup and saucer was made by Union Porcelain Works to celebrate the centennial celebration in 1876 and was designed by artist Karl Müller. The cup is white with a gilded and embossed figure of Justice on the cup and a handle in the form of Liberty. Cabinet cups and saucers made by this company are rare and bring high prices.

JAPAN

Japan has produced some of the world's most beautiful ceramic art, and Satsuma is one of the most distinctive. Resembling aged ivory, Satsuma is a soft-paste porcelain characterized by a fine creamy crackle glaze. The finely detailed hand painting and gold enameling are what make Satsuma so treasured and sought after by discriminating collectors throughout the world. The detail on a Satsuma cup can be so elaborate that it takes a magnifying lens to appreciate the beauty and workmanship.

Another unique Japanese ceramic is beginning to catch the attention of collectors. It is a pottery called Banko Ware or Banko-yaki. This ware originated in the late eighteenth century and is characterized by thin, natural unglazed clay, hand modeling, and brightly colored enamels. Various marbleized or tapestry techniques were often used. Many pieces of Banko pottery are decorated with scenes from nature, such as cherry blossoms, bamboo, peonies, peacocks, and cranes.

ENGLISH COMPANIES

In his column "Studying English Ceramics," *Antique Trader*, 6/12/96, Bill Saks says, "Nothing can compare with the workmanship and quality of the late-period demitasse from the noted Coalport and Royal Worcester factories."

Coalport

Coalport produced a line of magnificent ornamental cups and saucers in the 1880s that are expensive and highly prized by collectors. The cups and saucers are quite small in scale, the cups measuring 55mm in diameter (excluding the handle) and the saucers measuring 90mm. Frequently of the quatrefoil shape, the handles are rustic, twig, or molded as coral. Colors are often a rich cobalt blue or gold, embellished with white, gold, coral, or

turquoise enameled designs and jeweling. Some have elaborately hand-painted scenic or floral reserves.

Royal Worcester

The quality of porcelains made at Worcester during the nineteenth century was exceptional. Cabinet pieces were richly painted and gilded. During the 1870s magnificent porcelains in the Japanese style were produced. Then followed pieces made and decorated in the Chinese, Persian, Indian, and Florentine styles. One of Royal Worcester's greatest triumphs was the remarkably reticulated pieces perfected by George Owens in the 1890s. The piercing was done when the piece was in the greenware stage, before biscuit firing. The work was painstaking, and the slightest error was irreparable.

Pieces completed by Owens were lace-like, delicate, and fragile, with every tiny shaped aperture separately pierced.

Another reason why Royal Worcester produced such high quality porcelains is the number of outstanding artists working for them. The company believed that every porcelain shape was intended above all to act as a canvas for fine painting. Boxed demitasse sets decorated by well-known artists were made c. 1880 – 1920 and are highly desirable. They might be sold intact or broken up, depending on the condition of the box and the cups and saucers.

Derby

In *Miller's Antiques Encyclopedia*, Judith Miller says, "In terms of quality, Derby cups or cans and saucers are so highly regarded that they began to rival the rich cabinet wares made at the factories of Meissen, Paris and Vienna." William Duesbury opened the Derby Works in Derby, England, in 1755. The specialty of Derby was cabinet wares, particularly cans and saucers and cabaret sets. They were too expensive to use and were intended purely to display. Landscapes, figures, birds, and fruit were painted in panels or reserves by outstanding artists. William Billingsley worked for Derby in the late eighteenth and early nineteenth centuries and was probably one of the greatest of all English flower painters. During the early nineteenth century, Derby excelled at copying the colorful patterns inspired by old Japanese Imari wares.

Minton

Established in 1873, Minton made magnificent dessert and tea services, many of which were decorated with ground colors reminiscent of Sevres with ornate gilding and extremely well-painted panels. Minton made porcelain copies of many Japanese and Chinese materials, including cloisonné wares. They used rich turquoise or pink enamel as a background, against which the designs were outlined in gold.

Coffee cup and saucer.

Ahrenfeldt, Charles & Son, c. 1886 – 1910.

Fragonard shape; large hand-painted roses, gilt leaves. (See mark #3.)

$100.00 – 125.00.

Small demitasse cup and saucer.

Dresden, Carl Thieme, c. 1901 – 1920.

Six-footed scalloped cup, branch handle; flowers encrusted outside cup and on bottom of saucer; hand-painted flowers inside.

$200.00 – 250.00.

Coffee cup and saucer.

Dresden, Donath & Co., c. 1893 – 1916.

Three-claw-footed cup with twisted snake handle; hand-painted garlands of flowers. Magnificent!

$350.00 – 400.00.

Rare trembleuse and saucer.

Dresden, Carl Thieme, c. 1920.

Scalloped cup with angular handle; hand-painted flowers.

$300.00 – 350.00.

Coffee cup and saucer.

Dresden, Lamm, A., c. 1887.

Fragonhard shape; magnificent hand-painted scene after "Geschmack," lady with four Cupids, beautiful beading, and raised gilt fleur-de-lis on pale yellow. A museum piece!

$550.00 – 650.00.

Reverse side of above cup.

Demitasse cup and saucer.

Dresden, Lamm, A., c. 1887 – 1891.

Straight-sided cup with loop handle; raised gilt decoration and celeste blue banding, hand-painted scene of robed woman with a hammer and chisel carving "Der Freundschaft Und Liebe" onto side of rock (friendship and love); gold silhouette on reverse. (See mark #33.)

$300.00 – 350.00.

Reverse side of above cup, showing silhouette.

Teacup and saucer.

Dresden, Klemm, R., c. 1902 – 1916.

Round cup with loop handle; scenic medallions on cobalt, gilt scrolls. (See mark #32.)

$150.00 – 200.00.

Teacup and saucer.

Dresden, Lamm, A., c. 1887 – 1891.

Royal Flute cup with twisted, divided feathered handle, saucer bowl; hand gilding on cobalt, wonderful hand-painted portrait medallion on cup and in saucer.

$300.00 – 350.00.

Demitasse cup and saucer.

Dresden, Lamm, A., c. 1887 – 1891.

Footed cup with magnificent gilt bird handle; luscious gilt decoration on cobalt blue, gold beading, and pearl jeweling.

$350.00 – 375. 00.

Demitasse cup and saucer.

KPM (Kings Porcelain Manufactory), c. 1890s.

Bute cup with unusual handle; beautiful vivid hand-painted flowers, heavy gilt decoration.

$350.00 – 400.00.

Demitasse cup and saucer.

Hutschenreuther, C. M., c. 1925 – 1941.

Quatrefoil cup with double gilt ring handle; yellow with gilt interior. (See mark #47.)

$60.00 – 75.00.

Group of four cups and saucers like above, different ground colors.

Demitasse cup and saucer.

Kuba, Josef, Carlsbad, c. 1900 – 1945.

Footed cup with high coiled handle; magnificent hand-gilt work of scrolls and playful figures and fairies on dark red. (See mark #52.)

$100.00 – 125.00.

Demitasse cup and saucer.

Meissen, c. 1850 – 1924.

Slightly flared, footed cup, loop handle with flat thumb rest; heavy gold molded leaf design on white.

$175.00 – 225.00.

Demitasse cup and saucer.

Meissen, c. 1850 – 1924.

Slightly flared, footed cup, loop handle with flat thumb rest; cobalt with gilt molded leaf design.

$200.00 – 250.00.

Teacup, saucer, and plate.

Meissen, c. 1924 – 1934.

Scalloped cup and saucer, feathered kicked loop handle; cobalt and gilt rim, lovely hand-painted flowers.

$300.00 – 350.00.

Demitasse cup and saucer.

Meissen, c. 1934 – present.

Scalloped footed cup with ornate gilt handle; heavy gilt decoration on cobalt and white.

$200.00 – 250.00.

Demitasse cup and saucer.

Meissen, c. 1860 – 1924.

Twelve-paneled cup with London-style handle; alternating panels of colorful hand-painted flowers and gilt decoration.

$200.00 – 250.00.

Coffee cup and saucer.

Rosenthal, c. 1901 – 1956.

Footed cup with gilt bird handle; magnificent heavy hand gilt scrolling.

$250.00 – 300.00.

Coffee cup and saucer.

Rosenthal, c. 1908 – 1953.

Fragonhard cup; medallions of hand-painted flowers on cobalt blue, artist signed.

$150.00 – 200.00.

Demitasse cup and saucer.

Rosenthal, c. 1908 – 1953.

Rounded cup with gilt inside, square handle; white flowers on green band.

$50.00 – 75.00.

Demitasse cup and saucer.

Rosenthal, c. 1901 – 1933.

Cup with scalloped foot, scalloped saucer; gilt stars on black ground.

$90.00 – 125.00.

Demitasse cup and saucer.

Schafer & Vater, Rudolstadt, c. 1896 – 1962.

Figural cup in shape of pale blue rose.

$75.00 – 100.00.

Demitasse cup and saucer.

Beehive mark, c. 1895 – 1920.

Can with loop handle; hand-painted portrait medallion; couple playing music, gilt beading and white jeweling.

$125.00 – 175.00.

Coffee cup and saucer.

Beehive decorating mark, Rosenthal blank, c. 1891 – 1907.

Fragonard cup; hand-painted portrait medallion of lady with cupid, gilding, jeweling, and gold beading on dark red; lovely cabinet cup.

$250.00 – 300.00.

Demitasse cup and saucer.

Beehive mark, c. 1890s.

Bute cup with loop handle, gilding inside cup; artist signed, hand-painted children in singing activities, "GESANG."

$250.00 – 275.00.

Coffee cup and saucer.

Beehive, probably Joseph Riedl, c. 1890 – 1918.

Cup on three paw feet with twisted snake handle, raised well in saucer; portrait medallion with hand gilded decoration.

$100.00 – 125.00.

Demitasse cup and saucer.

Austria, c. 1920s.

Quatrefoil cup with backwards "C" handle; silver overlay on pink.

$125.00 – 175.00.

Covered chocolate cup and saucer.

Capodimonte, c. 1870.

Magnificent two-handled covered chocolate cup with ornate handles, putti finial on lid; figures and scenes in relief.

$500.00 – 600.00.

Same cup as above, showing detail of saucer.

Demitasse cup and saucer.

Capodimonte, c. 1890.

Cup with twisted twig handle; hand-painted relief decoration of cavorting Cupids, crest on saucer.

$125.00 – 175.00.

Chocolate cup with lid and two handles.

Limoges, c. 1900.

Can with two ornate gilt handles, deep saucer, pine-cone finial; decorated in Samson style.

$250.00 – 275.00.

Teacup, saucer, and dessert plate.

Limoges blank, decorated by Le Tallec, Paris, for Carole Stupeel, New York, c. 1950.

Round low cup with fat loop handle, gilt foot; white enameled scrollwork on pink. (See mark #71.)

$300.00 – 350.00.

Chocolate cup and saucer.

Limoges, c. 1890s – 1914.

Slightly flared cup with scalloped base and saucer, wishbone handle; gilt flowers on cobalt.

$125.00 – 150.00.

Chocolate cup and saucer.

Limoges, unreadable mark, L. S. & S., c. 1890 – 1925.

Eight-fluted cup with loop handle; beautiful fern decoration.

$125.00 – 150.00.

Chocolate cup and saucer.

Limoges, Coiffe & L. S. & S., c. 1891 – 1914.

Cup flared at bottom two-thirds, rustic handle; gilt on rim, band of dark red, medallions of flowers, beading. (See mark #58.)

$125.00 – 150.00.

Coffee cup and saucer.

Limoges, T. & V., c. 1892 – 1907.

Fragonhard shape; hand-painted floral medallions on green.

$100.00 – 125.00.

Trembleuse.

Insect mark, possibly Limoges, LaPorte, Raymond, home decorated, c. 1891 – 1897.

Large bucket-shaped can with deep well, divided stem handle; wonderful hand-painted scene of Spanish lady in garden with flowers outlined in gilt on saucer, gentleman serenading her on cup, framed in gold.

$150.00 – 200.00.

Another view of above trembleuse.

Chocolate cup and saucer.

Limoges, L. S. & S., c. 1890 – 1920.

Beautiful fluted cup with gilt wavy mold at bottom, ornate handle; hand-gilt decoration and hand-painted flowers.

$100.00 – 125.00.

Snack set.

Claude de France, Tours, France, c. 1880 – 1920s.

Cup with loop handle, gold wash inside, saucer with scalloped tray; jeweled Persian motif on cobalt.

$225.00 – 275.00.

Coffee can and saucer.

Sevres, c. 1870 – 1890s.

Bucket-shaped can with unusual handle; medallion with hand-painted Cupids outlined with "pearl jeweling," blue ground.

$400.00 – 500.00.

Another view of above cup showing handle.

Coffee cup and saucer.

Sevres, c. 1814 – 1824.

Empire shape; bands of hand-painted flowers on gilt, scenic monochrome painting on front of cup.

$600.00 – 800.00.

Another view of above cup and saucer.

Covered chocolate cup and saucer.

Unidentified French company, c. 1875 – 1890.

Tall can with deep saucer, unusual ornate handles, gilt flower bud finial; magnificent enameled stylized flowers on cobalt blue.

$350.00 – 400.00.

Demitasse cup and saucer.

Ceramic Art Co., c. 1894 – 1906.

Ribbed quatrefoil cup; floral enameling in two shades of gold on pale pink.

$125.00 – 150.00.

Demitasse cup and saucer.

Lenox, c. 1930s.

Bute cup with loop handle; hand-painted plums by J. Nosek.

$100.00 – 125.00.

Teacup and saucer.

Pickard, c. 1912 – 1918.

Round cup with loop handle; Modern Conventional signed Robert Hessler. (See mark #88.)

$200.00 – 250.00.

Teacup and saucer.

Willets Manufacturing Company, c. 1885 – 1909.

Deeply scalloped, waisted footed cup with gilt broken loop handle with spur; exquisite decoration of gold paste leaves and sponged gold work on Belleek body; jeweled flowers outside cup.

$250.00 – 300.00.

Teacup and saucer.

Japanese Kutani, c. 1900 – 1920.

Molded and scalloped cup with rustic handle; magnificent intricate hand-painted butterfly design.

$200.00 – 250.00.

Teacup and saucer.

Japanese Banko Ware, cartouche, late nineteenth century.

Cup and saucer slightly crimped in five sections, flower bud on stem handle; hand-enameled flowers and yellow berries on thin walled earthenware. (See mark #8.)

$150.00 – 175.00.

Demitasse cup and saucer.

Japanese Banko Ware, c. 1930s.

Quatrefoil cup and saucer, kicked loop handle; tapestry pattern.

$100.00 – 125.00.

Chocolate cup and saucer.

Unmarked, pre-Nippon, c. 1880s.

Five-fluted cup flaring out at bottom, unusual square handle; medallions of roses, exquisite beading covering all other areas of the cup and saucer.

$175.00 – 200.00.

Chocolate cup and saucer.

Unmarked, pre-Nippon, c. 1880s.

Six-fluted cup flaring out at bottom, unusual square handle; medallions of hand-painted flowers bordered by gilt scrolls.

$75.00 – 100.00.

Teacup and saucer.

Unmarked, probably Nippon, c. 1890 – 1921.

Footed cup, scalloped saucer, ornate handle; lovely pink roses on gold ground.

$150.00 – 175.00.

Teacup and saucer.

Japanese, probably unmarked Nippon, c. 1900.

Round footed cup with wide loop handle; lavishly decorated with gold, cobalt, and roses, beading.

$125.00 – 150.00.

Teacup and saucer.

Unmarked, probably Japan, c. 1930 – 1950.

Figural shell-shaped cup and saucer; inserted tea bag holder; coral-like handle extending to make four feet for cup; hand-painted flowers and leaf decoration.

$75.00 – 100.00.

Demitasse cup and saucer.

Satsuma, Japanese cartouche, late nineteenth century.

Round cup with magnificent scaly dragon handle; heavy enameled flowers.

$250.00 – 275.00.

Small teacup and saucer.

Aynsley, c. 1891 – 1910.

Scalloped and flared cup with broken loop handle; magnificent Persian-type floral design with rich cobalt, red, and gold.

$125.00 – 150.00.

Teacup and saucer.

Aynsley, c. 1891 – 1920s.

Footed cup with rare colorful butterfly handle; scenic cup and saucer with portrait of woman on cup. (See mark #4.)

$250.00 – 275.00.

Demitasse cup and saucer.

Coalport, made for Bailey, Banks & Biddle, c. 1881 – 1890.

Swirled cup with gold twig handle; heavy gold enameled leaves on dark red. (See mark #15.)

$200.00 – 250.00.

Demitasse cup and saucer.

Coalport, c. 1891 – 1920.

Bute cup with loop handle; gold inside cup; white roses with cobalt blue leaves on gold and white. (See mark #16.)

$250.00 – 275.00.

Teacup and saucer.

Coalport, c. 1948 – 1959.

Lovely swirled, scalloped, and beaded mold on cup and saucer, loop handle; swirled coral petals with gilt accents. (See mark #17.)

$125.00 – 150.00.

Teacup and saucer.

Copelands-Spode, c. 1891+.

Flared and scalloped cup with pinched loop handle with large thumb rest and spur; hand-gilded scrolls and flowers on cobalt blue. (See mark #22.)

$125.00 – 150.00.

Demitasse cup and saucer

Royal Crown Derby, c. 1891.

Bute cup with square handle; heavy gilt flowers on pale yellow, gold wash inside cup.

$250.00 – 275.00.

Demitasse cup and saucer.

Crown Derby, c. 1888.

Straight-sided cup with ring handle; heavy gilt butterfly and flowers on red. (See mark #25.)

$150.00 – 175.00.

Small teacup and saucer.

Royal Doulton, c. 1902 – 1956.

Ribbed cup with loop handle, gilt inside cup; lovely gold work on pink and white.

$150.00 – 200.00.

Coffee cup and saucer.

Royal Doulton, c. 1922 – 1956.

Fragonard cup; hand-gilded flowers and scrollwork on dark red.

$100.00 – 125.00.

Demitasse cup and saucer.

Royal Doulton, c. 1902 – 1922.

Can with loop handle, gold inside cup; pink and white with gold scrollings and beading.

$150.00 – 200.00.

Demitasse cup and saucer.

Royal Doulton, c. 1920s.

Scalloped cup with angular handle, gilt interior; cobalt ground with gilt leafy garland and urns.

$225.00 – 275.00.

Teacup and saucer.

Hammersley & Co., c. 1912 – 1939.

Footed scalloped and slightly ribbed cup with rustic broken loop handle, deep saucer; heavy gold floral paste on green.

$125.00 – 150.00.

Same cup and saucer as above, on yellow ground.

Teacup and saucer.

Hammersley, c. 1912 – 1939.

Fluted cup with ornate "C" handle; floral medallions on cobalt blue; beautiful hand-gilt work. (See mark #42.)

$100.00 – 125.00.

Coffee cup and saucer.

Hammersley, for Ovington Bros., New York, c. 1887 – 1912.

Fragonhard-shaped cup; roses and daisies on gilt, gorgeous! (See mark #41.)

$150.00 – 175.00.

Demitasse cup and saucer.

Old Hall Works, Ltd., made for F. Lehudlze & Co., Cincinnati, Ohio, c. 1886 – 1902.

Footed and scalloped cup and saucer, ornate handle; medallions of flowers on gilt, green fleur-de-lis pattern.

$95.00 – 115.00.

Demitasse cup and saucer.

Royal Worcester, 1924.

Gilt design on cobalt with pearl jeweling, gold inside cup.

$350.00 – 400.00.

Demitasse cup and saucer.

Royal Worcester, c. 1924.

Cup with gilt interior, foot rim and loop handle; exquisite hand-painted peacocks signed by R. H. Austin.

$400.00 – 450.00.

Boxed set of above.

$1,800.00 – 2,400.00.

Demitasse cup and saucer.

Royal Worcester, c. 1917.

Cup with gilt foot rim, gilt loop handle, gold inside cup; dark green with band of pearl and gold jeweling.

$150.00 – 175.00.

Demitasse cup and saucer.

Royal Worcester, c. 1927.

Bute cup with loop handle; heavy gilt and jeweling on white and black ground. (See mark #120.)

$200.00 – 225.00.

Demitasse cup and saucer.

Royal Worcester, c. 1887.

Bucket-shaped can with decorated loop handle; hand-painted flowers outlined in gold.

$150.00 – 175.00.

Demitasse cup and saucer.

Royal Worcester, c. 1902.

Cup with loop handle; bands of yellow and blue ground, red jeweling.

$100.00 – 125.00.

Demitasse cup and saucer.

Unmarked, c. 1890 – 1920.

Unusual trefoil shape with question-mark handle; heavily enameled daisies, gilt leaves on pink ground.

$75.00 – 100.00.

ELEGANT DINNERWARE SERVICES

Cups and saucers from the elegant dinnerware services of the late nineteenth and twentieth centuries provide much variety and offer good value for the collector.

MEISSEN

The first matching dinnerware sets were made by the Meissen Company in Germany in the 1720s. Flowers were used copiously in Meissen dinnerware. In 1745 the company used German flowers painted after nature, and these floral patterns are still being used today. Meissen cups and saucers are highly prized and sought after by collectors the world over. When you pick up a piece, you can see the beauty and feel the quality of this hand-painted, finely decorated porcelain.

DRESDEN DECORATING STUDIOS

Between 1850 and 1914 as many as 200 decorating studios evolved in and around Dresden, Germany, creating a "Dresden" style, a mixture of Meissen and Vienna. This decorating style was a simple painting of life-like flowers on a pure white background with gilt scroll borders.

Helena Wolfsohn had one of the most prolific decorating workshops in the late nineteenth century. Wolfsohn specialized in painting tea and coffee wares, often copying Meissen. The decoration was typically divided into quarters with figures in landscapes in the style of Watteau, alternating with floral panels. Other Dresden workshops included Donath & Co., Richard Klemm, Adolph Hammann, and A. Lamm. Lamm produced some exquisite hand-painted cups and saucers of the highest quality.

CARL SCHUMANN PORCELAIN FACTORY

Founded by Heinrich Schumann in 1881 and still in operation today, the Carl Schumann Porcelain Factory produces coffee and tea sets, dinner services, and decorative items. Schumann's popular dinnerware sets in the "Dresden Flowers" patterns such as Chateau and Empress are quite popular with collectors today. Many pieces are reticulated with gilt trim. The florals are not hand-painted, such as those done by the Dresden studios, but are good quality transfers.

LORENZ HUTSCHENREUTHER

Lorenz Hutschenreuther established the first china factory in Selb, Germany, in 1857. While the early German factories such as Meissen and KPM produced porcelain for the courts and noblemen, private factories such as Hutschenreuther made china available to the general public. Many of these dinnerware sets are richly decorated in underglaze cobalt blue and embellished with gold and platinum. One of their most well-known patterns is the Blue Onion.

The company used an export mark, Black Knight, which was registered in the United States by Graham and Zenger, New York, c. 1925 – 1941. Cups and saucers with this mark often have outstanding decoration.

ROSENTHAL

Also located in Selb, Germany, is the Rosenthal factory. Philip Rosenthal got his start by buying whiteware blanks from Hutschenreuther, decorating them and selling them door-to-door. He opened his factory in 1879. The high quality workmanship and simplicity of design made Rosenthal's dinnerware highly acclaimed.

In 1961 Rosenthal introduced the Studio Line decor. Pieces in this line reflect a new interest in simplicity and the restraint of modern design. Rosenthal's most successful dinner service is Maria, first offered in 1914. It sold in the millions and is still offered today, marked "Rosenthal Classic." Other popular patterns are Iris, Botticelli, Donatello, and Moss Rose. Most Rosenthal china is decorated with a combination of transfer and overpainting. The exquisite gilding is usually hand applied.

JOHANN HAVILAND

The firm began operation in 1907 in Waldershof, Germany, producing hotel china, everyday china, and fine china. They were sold to Rosenthal China in 1937 and began producing fine china for export. This dinnerware was marked "Johann Haviland, Bavaria, Germany," and includes some fine cobalt and gold beverage and dessert sets.

R.S. PRUSSIA

The porcelain dinnerware manufactured by the Schlegelmilch brothers in Suhl and Silesia in the 1860s is especially treasured today. The R.S. Prussia molds are some of the most fascinating aspects of this porcelain. Many are ornately formed with scrollwork, delicate flowers, or other shapes as part of the mold. Decoration was usually transfer designs with hand-applied gold enameling. Lovely soft pastel background colors were used with satiny, pearlized, or glossy finishes. Unusual molded handles can be found on cups, such as the question mark and curved loop. Popular themes include floral, animal, portrait, and scenic.

LIMOGES, FRANCE

The most popular dinnerware in the mid- to late nineteenth century was Limoges porcelain. In *Godden's Guide to European Porcelains*, Geoffrey Godden says, "Limoges is to France as Stoke-on-Trent is to England — the center of the ceramic industry." Limoges is about 200 miles southwest of Paris and owes its prominence in the field of hard-paste porcelain production in France to the abundance of natural resources. The period of the mid-to late 1800s was the golden age for the Limoges porcelain industry.

The Haviland Company, organized in 1840, was one of the most famous companies located in Limoges, and their elegant dinner services graced the White House dining room tables for many years in the nineteenth century. As many as 60,000 chinaware patterns were designed by Haviland. Arlene, Dick, and Donna Schlieger have published six books with detailed drawings of over 1,200 patterns, known as Schlieger numbers.

Cups and saucers from dinnerware, demitasse, and chocolate sets from any of the companies located in and around Limoges, France, are eagerly collected because they offer a tremendous variety of shapes and decorations and are usually very affordable. Even the blanks are interesting; many have scrollwork, beading, scalloped borders, or fancy handles. Collectors look for the hand-painted examples, preferably by French factories. Floral decor, especially the rose, is the most frequent decoration. Some cups and saucers have deep, vivid colors, while others, especially those by Theodore Haviland, have delicate pastel coloring. Many are prized because of their rich gold embellishments and dainty molded shapes.

ROYAL COPENHAGEN PORCELAIN FACTORY

The Royal Copenhagen factory was established in 1775, and its famous three wavy line trademark symbolizes the Sound, the Great Belt, and the Little Belt of Denmark. Along with figures and Christmas plates, their specialty is dinnerware. Royal Copenhagen's most well-known pattern, Blue Flute, is of Chinese origin and was created in 1780. It has three

edge forms: smooth edge, closed lace edge, and perforated lace edge. Another famous pattern, Blue Flower, was first designed in 1775. The blue bouquets are still painted by hand and include roses, tulips, poppies, and carnations. Each piece carries the signature of the painter. There are three different versions of Blue Flower: angular, curved, and braided.

BING & GRONDAHL

Bing & Grondahl is another outstanding porcelain company, established in Copenhagen, Denmark, in 1853. The company is well known for their production of the first Christmas plate in 1895. They also produce figurines and fine dinnerware, and each piece is signed with either the artist's name or initials. The Seagull pattern is popular with collectors.

HEREND

Herend porcelain was founded in 1826 by V. Stengl. Around 1839 Mór Fischer bought the company and led it to fame with his reproductions of Chinese porcelain. At the Great Exhibition in 1851 at the Crystal Palace in London, the beautiful dinner, tea, and coffee services exhibited by Fischer were admired by all and brought worldwide recognition to the Herend company.

Early Herend tableware was influenced by Meissen decoration with basketweave and pierced borders and the typical floral bouquet as a central motif. Most Herend porcelain is painted by hand by talented porcelain painters. Throughout the years, Herend's philosophy has been to preserve old traditions while honoring the spirit of the times.

One of the most popular Herend patterns is the Rothschild Birds — a series of 12 different multicolored birds depicted in a variety of ways, such as singing, perched in a tree, or in pairs surrounded by tiny insects. The ornate Chinese Bouquet pattern, found in green, blue, rust, and pink, is also a collector favorite.

IRISH BELLEEK

David McBirney and Robert Armstrong founded the Belleek Pottery Company in County Fermanagh, Ireland, in 1857. Using local clay deposits, they soon produced Belleek Parian china which was extremely thin and light with a creamy ivory surface and pearl-like luster. Today the dinnerware is still hand crafted, just as it was more than 100 years ago. Shamrock, Tridacna, Neptune, and Mask are but a few of the eagerly collected tea ware patterns, the Shamrock being the most popular.

Afternoon tea with Irish Belleek tea set in Neptune pattern, postcard produced by Lakeland Design, Bailieborough.

THE UNITED STATES

AMERICAN BELLEEK

In the United States cups and saucers in American Belleek are of exceptional quality and sure to please the most discriminating collector. From 1883 until 1930, several potteries located in New Jersey and Ohio manufactured a type of china similar to the famous Irish Belleek parian. This luxury tableware is considered the highest achievement of the American porcelain industry.

LENOX, INC.

Today Lenox, Inc., is the only one of the companies manufacturing American Belleek still in existence, and it is the leader of American dinnerware production. Collectors seek early cups and saucers with naturalistic themes and raised gold and pastel matte colors.

PICKARD, INC.

Pickard, Inc. was established in Edgerton, Wisconsin, in 1894 as a decorating firm. The company bought china blanks, mainly from European firms such as Limoges, and decorated the pieces with fruits, floral, birds, portraits, and scenes with gold embellishments. In his book *Collector's Encyclopedia of Pickard China*, the late Alan B. Reed says, "If there was a high period for Pickard's hand-painted china, the 1902 – 1918 period was that."

Early designs were colorful and naturalistic, resembling European china of the period. Soon porcelain artists developed stylized designs named Conventional, which reflect the Art Nouveau movement. Another popular stylized pattern is Aura Argenta Linear. Today the market is strong for Pickard artist-signed cups and saucers. Other decorating studios of the period, such as J. H. Stouffer and the Osbourne Art Studio, are also attracting collector attention.

SYRACUSE CHINA

Syracuse China began operation as the Onondaga Pottery Company in 1871 located in Syracuse, New York. By 1890 the factory was making a vitrified china that was white, thin, translucent, and stronger than any European porcelain. In 1893 "Syracuse China" was introduced and awarded a medal at the World Exhibition in Chicago. During the next 60 years it continued to expand, producing lovely dinnerware until 1970, when the consumer division closed.

AMERICAN CHINA PAINTING

The development of china painting as an art form in the United States is said to have had its roots in the Arts and Crafts Movement in the late nineteenth century. Instead of relying on foreign goods, Americans became interested in their own arts and crafts. Another important factor was the increasingly active role in the arts which American women were embracing. China painting, a delicate and relatively neat and clean art, held great appeal for women. Middle class women could engage in it without compromising their husbands' social standings. It was also an occupation in which women from lower incomes could engage rather than going into a "sweat shop" environment. For both classes of women china painting offered an opportunity for creative expression.

In May 1899, Adelaide Alsop Robineau, a respected porcelain artist, and her husband, Samuel, began publishing *Keramic Studio Magazine*. She was perhaps the one person responsible for propelling the momentum of china painting into the twentieth century. The magazine achieved immediate success, and by 1905 it was estimated that there were some 20,000 professional china decorators. Much of the porcelain white ware used by these artists was imported from Limoges, France. Cups and saucers that are home decorated are often quite beautiful and unique, and should be judged on their individual merit.

JAPAN

NIPPON

Japan produced lovely Nippon beverage sets during the period from 1891 to 1921 in a variety of shapes, designs, and decorations. Much of the porcelain was hand painted with gold embellishments and beading and is enthusiastically collected today.

NORITAKE

The Noritake Company, founded in 1904 in Nagoya, Japan, has devoted itself to making elegant china for dining room tables around the world. Even today the company is constantly refining its technologies and innovating new china ware. Perhaps the most popular Noritake pattern is the Azalea pattern which was a premium offered by Larkin Co.

KUTANI LITHOPHANES

A lithophane is a translucent porcelain

panel with an impressed design of which the detail is only visible when held up to the light. Lithophanes were made on teacups and demitasse cups in Japan in the 1920s and 1930s and are very popular with collectors today.

OCCUPIED JAPAN

Cups and saucers of nice quality were made in Japan from 1947 – 1952 and are marked "Occupied Japan." Miniatures were made in the Japanese Imari pattern, and teacups and saucers were made in the Capodimonte style, as well as ordinary dinnerware patterns.

LEFTON

The Lefton China Company was established in Chicago, Illinois, by George Z. Lefton, a native of Hungary. The company originated as a marketing company of good quality porcelain products mainly made in Japan. Lefton participated in the design of many pieces produced in the beginning years of his company.

THE MOST POPULAR DINNERWARE PATTERNS

WILLOW

Willow is the most popular tableware pattern ever made. The first was put on English porcelain in 1780 at Caughley Pottery. Thomas Minton, one of their decorators, adapted the design from Oriental wares. The colors vary from a fine old blue to an almost purple shade. Black and even multicolored willow ware may be found, but the pattern is basically the same — the mandarin's pagoda, the willow tree, the bridge with runaway lovers crossing it, the boat that took them to their island, and the clouds they turned into. Connie Rogers, author of *Willow Pattern China Made in USA*, says that over 200 English potteries produced the willow pattern, as well as 45 different American companies. Many other countries produced willow pattern china as well.

ONION

The best known and most copied porcelain decoration created by Meissen is the Blue Onion pattern. Designed in the early 1700s, it was based on a Chinese pattern from the Ming Dynasty and got its name from a stylized peach that resembled an onion. More than 60 European and Oriental companies used this decoration, and many cup and saucer collectors hunt for examples of the different onion styles.

IMARI

Imari was named after the Japanese port from where the porcelain was shipped in the late seventeeth century. The decoration was copied from textiles popular at the time. The pattern is divided into panels, featuring iron-red, underglaze blue, and gilding. Royal Crown Derby is well known for its Imari patterns. The two most popular are #2451 and #1138, and they are both still in production and expensive. These patterns were copied by many companies.

OLD COUNTRY ROSES

This colorful pattern was created by Royal Albert in 1962 and designed by Harold Holdcroft. Various tableware and decorative items have been made in this popular pattern.

SPODE BLUE ITALIAN

This was a famous 1816 blue and white design, probably based on an Old Master painting. It shows ruins, a castle in the background, houses, and figures.

NAPOLEON IVY

This pattern was made by Wedgwood in 1815. It is a simple border of ivy leaves on creamware. Napoleon is said to have used a service in this pattern while in exile.

OTHER DINNERWARE ITEMS

BREAKFAST SETS

In England special breakfast sets were made in the 1920s and 1930s, usually for one or two people. They usually included a teapot, hot water pot, milk jug, sugar bowl, cereal bowl, cups, and saucers, all in matching patterns.

Sometimes a tray and toast rack were included.

BOUILLON CUPS AND SAUCERS

These are double-handled cups measuring 3½" in diameter and 2½" high and are similar to teacups and saucers. They were used to serve clear broths and sometimes had lids to keep the soup hot. Lidded bouillons are hard to find.

CREAM SOUPS AND SAUCERS

These cups are also double handed but are shallow and wider than bouillons and vary from 4 ½" to 5" in diameter and are 2" in height.

SNACK SETS

Snack sets are also called tea and biscuit sets, hospitality sets, sandwich sets, and tennis or tiffen sets in England. They are cups and tray-type saucers that are large enough to serve a light snack or sandwich. They were popular for early morning tea in bed or casual entertaining. Snack sets originated in the 1890s and remained popular until the 1970s.

Snack sets were made from ceramics or glass. The early porcelain sets marked "Limoges" or "Nippon" were quite ornate and are eagerly collected. They were also sold as bridge sets from the 1930s through the 1950s, and include eight cups, eight plates with cup indentation, a matching teapot or coffee pot, and a sugar and creamer.

Teacup, saucer, and plate.

Alka-Kunst Alboth & Kaiser, Bavaria, Germany, c. 1927 – 1953.

Round cup with ring handle; red and gold decoration with gold highlights.

$50.00 – 75.00.

Teacup and saucer.

C. Tielsch & Co., Altwasser, Germany, c. 1875 – 1935.

Footed cup with curled loop handle; hand-painted orchids on pale green, artist signed.

$45.00 – 60.00.

Teacup and saucer.

Dresden, Richard Klemm, c. 1888 – 1916.

Quatrefoil cup; broken loop handle with thumb rest; alternating hand-painted panels of figures on white and flowers on pink; gold decor on rim.

$125.00 – 150.00.

Demitasse cup and saucer.

Dresden, Donath & Co., 1893 – 1916.

Footed cup with high curled loop handle; raised well on saucer; hand-painted flowers, gilt cross hatch designs on rims.

$100.00 – 125.00.

Demitasse cup and saucer.

Dresden, Helena Wolfsohn, c. 1886.

Rounded cup and saucer with loop handle, gilt dots; hand-painted flowers. (See mark #36.)

$85.00 – 115.00.

Coffee can and saucer.

Dresden, Donath & Co., c. 1893 – 1916.

Swirled can and saucer, loop handle; lovely hand-painted flowers.

$100.00 – 125.00.

Teacup and saucer.

Dresden, Wissman, c. 1887 – 1890.

Scalloped cup on four-part feathered foot, slightly kicked loop handle with feathered thumb rest; exquisite hand-painted flowers. (See mark #34.)

$125.00 – 150.00.

Demitasse cup and saucer.

Dresden, Helena Wolfsohn, c. 1886.

Unusual twisted and scalloped can with wishbone handle; hand-painted flowers.

$100.00 – 125.00.

Teacup and saucer.

Dresden, Lamm, A., c. 1887 – 1891.

Ribbed cup with braided handle with gilt oval dots; band of hand-painted flowers on white, pink ribbing on bottom.

$150.00 – 175.00.

Demitasse cup and saucer.

Hutschenreuther, C. M., decorated by Black Knight, c. 1925 – 1941.

Straight-sided cup with angular gilt handle; band of fruit transfer, heavy etched band of gold.

$60.00 – 75.00.

Demitasse cup and saucer.

Hutschenreuther, C. M., Black Knight, c. 1925 – 1941.

Straight cup with angular handle; band of turquoise with medallions containing vases of flowers, bands of gold.

$40.00 – 55.00.

Teacup, saucer, and dessert plate.

Hutschenreuther, L., c. 1928 – 1943.

Cup with scalloped foot and ornate handle; gilt flowers on coral. (See mark #49.)

$60.00 – 80.00.

Demitasse cup and saucer.

Hutschenreuther, c. 1887.

Straight molded cup with rustic handle; lovely hand-painted flowers. (See mark #48.)

$55.00 – 65.00.

Teacup and saucer.

KPM (Kings Porcelain Manufactory), c. 1882 – 1900.

Rounded cup with unusual fringed feet, ornate scrolled loop handle with feathered thumb rest; hand-painted flowers.

$125.00 – 150.00.

Coffee cup and saucer.

Meissen, c. 1924 – 1934.

Cup with swan handle; strewn flowers.

$175.00 – 195.00.

Demitasse cup and saucer.

Meissen, c. 1924 – 1934.

Royal flute cup; hand-painted roses.

$125.00 – 150.00.

Teacup and saucer.

Meissen, second quality, c. 1930s.

Royal Flute cup with deep saucer; rose painting.

$75.00 – 100.00.

Coffee cup and saucer.

Meissen, second quality, c. 1930s.

Royal Flute cup with deep saucer; rose painting.

$75.00 – 100.00.

Bouillon cup and saucer.

Meissen, second quality, c. 1924 – 1934.

Royal Flute shape with two twisted feather handles; rose painting. (See mark #76.)

$75.00 – 100.00.

Teacup and saucer.

Meissen, c. 1865 – 1887.

Blue Onion with gilt rims.

$125.00 – 150.00.

Demitasse cup and saucer.

Meissen, c. 1860 – 1924.

Cup in Royal Flute shape with divided feather handle; Blue Onion. (See mark #75.)

$85.00 – 100.00.

Teacup and saucer.

Meissen, c. 1860 – 1924.

Twelve-lobed cup with kicked loop handle with thumb rest; purple Indian with gold dots.

$250.00 – 300.00.

Coffee cup and saucer.

Meissen, c. 1860 – 1924.

Oval quatrefoil cup with pinched loop handle; purple Indian with gold dots.

$250.00 – 300.00.

Demitasse cup and saucer.

Meissen, c. 1860 – 1924.

Lovely lobed quatrefoil cup with wishbone handle; purple Indian with gold dots.

$250.00 – 300.00.

Teacup and saucer.

Mitterteich Porcelain Factory, U. S. Zone, Germany, c. 1945 – 1949.

Cup with scalloped foot and ornate handle; band of blue with gilt scrolls and jewels.

$45.00 – 60.00.

Breakfast cup and saucer.

M.Z. Austria (Moritz Zdekauer), c. 1900.

Round cup with loop handle; beautiful hand-painted flowers inside and out. (See mark #80.)

$50.00 – 75.00.

Teacup and saucer.

Nymphenburg (Royal Porcelain Manufactory, Nymphenberg), c. 1895.

Swirled cup and saucer, loop handle, delicate hand-painted flowers. (See mark #83.)

$75.00 – 100.00.

Teacup and saucer.

Maker unidentified, marked "Persian Ware, Germany," c. 1930s.

Rounded earthenware cup with fat loop handle; colorful hand-painted flowers. (See mark #87.)

$35.00 – 45.00.

Teacup, saucer, and plate.

Reichenbach Porcelainwork VEB, Germany, c. 1949 – 1968.

Round pedestal cup with reinforced ring handle; green bull's eye design on cream ground.

$50.00 – 75.00.

Demitasse cup and saucer.

Rosenthal, c. 1903 – 1953, made for Ovingtons.

Straight-sided cup with square handle; cobalt blue with hand decorated gilt work, floral transfer in center.

$40.00 – 55.00.

Teacup, saucer, and dessert plate.

Rosenthal blank, decorated by Julius H. Brauer Studio, c. 1911 – 1926.

Cup flared at bottom, triangular handle; light blue band with blue forget-me-nots.

$75.00 – 85.00.

Demitasse cup and saucer.

Rosenthal, U. S. Zone, c. 1945 – 1949.

Scalloped and footed cup with "ear" handle; Pompadour.

$50.00 – 60.00.

Teacup and saucer.

Rosenthal, c. 1949 – 1954.

Shallow footed cup with angular loop handle; scattered flowers on white.

$35.00 – 45.00.

Teacup, saucer, and dessert plate.

Rosenthal, c. 1950s.

Molded cup with unusual handle; San Souci pattern.

$75.00 – 100.00.

Teacup and saucer.

Rosenthal, c. 1901 – 1933.

Quatrefoil shape with coiled handle; Louis Philipp.

$60.00 – 85.00.

Coffee cup, saucer, and plate.

Rosenthal Studio Line, c. 1950s.

Pedestal cup with angular loop handle; leaf pattern. (See mark #92.)

$50.00 – 60.00.

Demitasse cup and saucer.

Rosenthal, dated 1938, home decorated in Denmark.

Shallow cup with slightly angular handle; gold clover on pale green.

$50.00 – 65.00.

Teacup and saucer.

Rosenthal, c. 1943 – 1952.

Footed, flared cup with unusual handle; Chippendale.

$40.00 – 55.00.

Teacup, saucer, and dessert plate.

Rosenthal, c. 1949 – 1954.

Footed cup with oval loop handle; band of deep cobalt with gilt scrolls and floral decoration.

$100.00 – 125.00.

Teacup and saucer.

Rosenthal, c. 1901 – 1933.

Cup with scalloping on bottom, unusual heart-shaped handle; hand-painted Iris pattern. (See mark #91.)

$40.00 – 55.00.

Coffee cup and saucer.

Royal Bayreuth (Porcelain Factory Tettau), c. 1902.

Fluted cup, scalloped at bottom, kidney-shaped handle; lovely mums, mixed decoration. (See mark #98.)

$50.00 – 65.00.

Chocolate cup and saucer.

R.S. Prussia, c. 1904 – 1938.

Fluted cup with angular handle; pink roses.

$75.00 – 100.00.

Teacup and saucer.

R.S. Prussia (Reinhold Schlegelmilch), c. 1904 – 1938.

Puffed-out quatrefoil cup with ornate handle; floral transfer, gilt, and beading at base. (See mark #105.)

$85.00 – 115.00.

Snack set.

Schonwald Porcelain Factory, Arzburg, Bavaria, c. 1920 – 1927.

Round cup with slightly rustic handle, amateur decorated with fruit in Pickard style.

$40.00 – 50.00.

Demitasse cup and saucer.

Schumann, Carl Porcelain Factory, c. 1918.

Twelve-ribbed cup and saucer; garlands of flowers with medallions of roses.

$30.00 – 40.00.

Teacup, saucer, and dessert plate.

Schumann, Carl, current mark.

Rounded, molded cup; scalloped saucer, loop handle with thumb rests; Dresden flowers. (See mark #109.)

$100.00 – 125.00.

Teacup and saucer.

Schumann, Carl, c. 1950s – present.

Molded cup, handle with thumb rest, scalloped saucer; Orlibe.

$30.00 – 40.00.

Demitasse cup and saucer.

Schumann, Carl, U. S. Zone, c. 1945 – 1949.

Straight cup with loop handle and low thumb rest; Dresden Flowers.

$45.00 – 60.00.

Demitasse cup and saucer.

Schumann, Carl, c. 1932.

Footed cup with coiled handle; Dresden style with alternate transfer panels of flowers and scenes. (See mark #108.)

$45.00 – 60.00.

Same style as above in different colors.

Demitasse cup and saucer.

Schumann, Carl, c. 1918 – 1929.

Slightly paneled cup with scalloped foot, broken loop handle, lovely scalloped and molded saucer; Garland. (See mark #107.)

$50.00 – 75.00.

Teacup, saucer, and dessert plate.

Schumann, Carl, U. S. Zone, c. 1945 – 1949.

Round cup with loop handle, unusual reticulated rim on saucer and plate; Empress.

$125.00 – 150.00.

Teacup and saucer.

Old Ivory, Silesia, c. 1890s.

Footed cup with interesting handle; pattern #15.

$60.00 – 75.00.

Teacup and saucer.

Old Ivory, Silesia, c. 1890s.

Footed cup with unusual handle; pattern #16.

$60.00 – 75.00.

Demitasse cup and saucer.

Silesia Porcelain Factory, c. 1890 – 1916.

Fragonhard shape; Dresden hand-painted flowers.

$75.00 – 100.00.

Teacup and saucer.

Tirschenreuth, Bavaria, c. 1903 – 1981.

Footed cup with unusual ornate handle; grapes and autumn leaves; mixed decoration.

$40.00 – 55.00.

Teacup, saucer, and dessert plate.

Tirschenreuth, Bavaria, c. 1969 – present.

Footed cup with angular loop handle; Christmas design of candles and holly.

$60.00 – 75.00.

Teacup and saucer.

Unidentified mark, Deusch Ich Scherzer, made in Germany, Bavaria, U. S. Zone, c. 1945 – 1949.

Round cup and saucer, fat loop handle; lovely silver overlay on pink.

$150.00 – 200.00.

Teacup and saucer.

Numbered, German, c. 1890 – 1910.

Molded cup on four feet, flared and ribbed at rim, square twig handle; raised gold flowers.

$30.00 – 40.00.

Teacup and saucer.

German, unmarked, c. 1890s.

Straight-sided cup with fat loop handle, ribbed saucer; star decoration trimmed in gold with raised gold beads in center and around star, gold raised flowers on side.

$35.00 – 45.00.

Teacup and saucer.

Numbered, probably German, c. 1900.

Flared and four-footed cup with unusual handle; pearlized, hand-painted peaches.

$30.00 – 40.00.

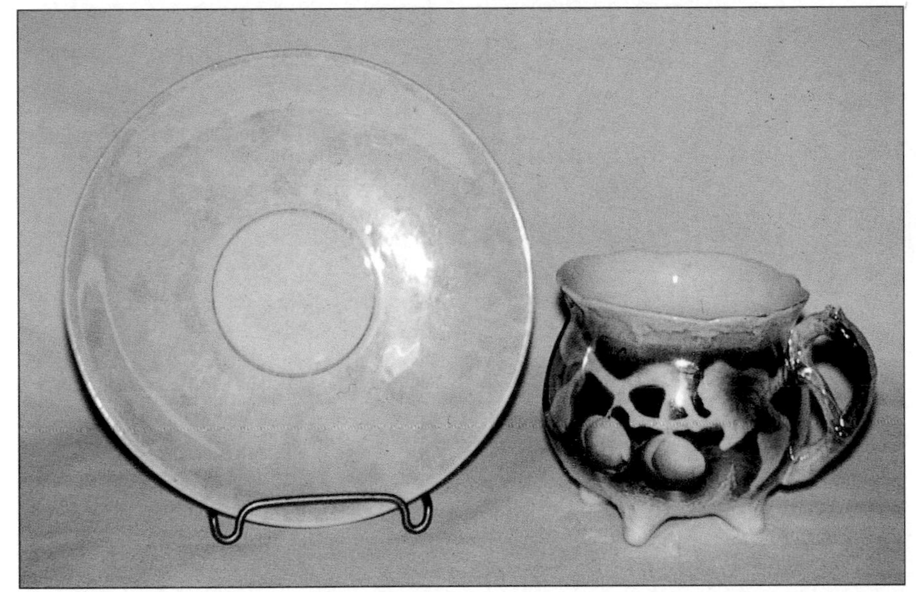

Teacup, saucer, and dessert plate.

Cup and saucer made by Union Porcelain, Czechoslovakia; dessert plate made by Thomas Company, Bavaria, probably home decorated, c. 1921 – 1927.

Rounded cup with unusual double-ring handle; hand-painted cherry blossoms, gilt trim.

$75.00 – 85.00.

Teacup and saucer.

Germany, unreadable china studio, c. 1920s.

Pretty rounded shape with unusual gilt handle; hand-painted flowers and gold band.

$30.00 – 40.00.

Demitasse cup and saucer.

Beehive mark, c. 1920 – 1930s.

Quatrefoil cup with loop handle; hand-painted floral decoration on inside and outside of cup.

$50.00 – 75.00.

Demitasse cup and saucer.

Beehive mark underglaze, c. 1920s.

Can with angular handle; Vienna-style decoration with eight portraits on saucer and five on cup.

$45.00 – 60.00.

Teacup, saucer, and plate.

Beehive mark and marked in gold, "Pizzoli Venezio," c. 1890 – 1918.

Round cup with gold inside, loop handle; hand-painted portraits, much gilt decoration.

$75.00 – 95.00.

Demitasse cup and saucer.

Von Schierholz, c. 1907.

Can with square handle; hand-painted flowers. (See mark #106.)

$60.00 – 75.00.

Teacup, saucer, and dessert plate.

Weimar, c. 1975 – present.

Tapered cup with scalloped foot, fancy handle, scalloped saucer with gilt rim; Katherine.

$75.00 – 100.00.

Teacup and saucer.

Herend, c. 1930s.

Scalloped cup and saucer with angular handle with flat thumb rest; gilt leafy design with two thin blue bands.

$75.00 – 95.00.

Coffee cup and saucer.

Herend, c. 1950s – present.

Scalloped cup and saucer, osier border, angular handle; Rothchild Bird pattern.

$125.00 – 150.00.

Teacup and saucer.

Herend, current mark.

Scalloped cup with osier border, angular handle; Chinese Rust Bouquet.

$100.00 – 125.00.

Demitasse cup and saucer.

Zsolnay, Pecs, Hungary, c. 1920 – 1930s.

Slightly flared cup with fancy broken loop handle; floral and butterfly transfer decoration.

$45.00 – 55.00.

Coffee cup and saucer.

Lomonosov Porcelain, Russia, c. 1930 – 1950s.

Tall fluted cup with small circular handle in middle of cup; pink flowers with insects.

$45.00 – 60.00.

Demitasse cup and saucer.

Rostrand, c. 1950 – present.

Straight cup with slightly scalloped saucer; floral transfer.

$40.00 – 50.00.

Demitasse cup and saucer.

Bing & Grondahl, c. 1952 – 1958.

Tapered cup with coiled angular handle; pate-sur-pate type blue and white floral design. (See mark #10.)

$40.00 – 50.00.

Teacup and saucer.

Bing & Grondahl, c. 1948.

Bute cup with sea gull handle; sea gull design #102. (See mark #9.)

$50.00 – 60.00.

Teacup, saucer, and dessert plate.

Royal Copenhagen Porcelain Factory, c. 1922 – present.

Bute cup with ring handle; brown floral transfer, hand gilded leaves.

$65.00 – 85.00.

Coffee cup and saucer.

Royal Copenhagen, c. 1922 – present.

Ribbed cup with ring handle; Plain Blue Lace pattern. (See mark #99.)

$60.00 – 90.00.

Coffee cup and saucer.

Gafle Porcelain Works, Sweden, c. 1950s.

Tapered coffee can with loop handle; stylized red transfer design.

$30.00 – 35.00.

Demitasse cup and saucer.

Porsgrund Porcelain Factory, Norway, current.

Slightly flared can with loop handle; floral transfer.

$30.00 – 35.00.

Demitasse cup and saucer.

Limoges, Haviland & Co., c. 1893 – 1930.

Molded cup with ornate handle, scalloped saucer; row of pink flowers.

$40.00 – 55.00.

Demitasse cup and saucer.

Limoges, L. S. & S., c. 1890 – 1925.

Cup ribbed at bottom, broken loop handle; blue shading, pink flowers.

$40.00 – 55.00.

Demitasse cup and saucer.

Limoges, Ahrenfeldt, c. 1894 – 1930.

Cup swirled at bottom, broken loop handle, saucer scalloped; bright red-orange flowers.

$35.00 – 45.00.

Demitasse cup and saucer.

Limoges, c. 1890s.

Fluted cup on four feet, leaf design.

$75.00 – 100.00.

Demitasse cup and saucer.

Limoges, Bernardaud & Co., c. 1914 – 1930.

Can with gilt loop handle; cobalt with gilt decoration; gilt inside. (See mark #57.)

$70.00 – 85.00.

Demitasse cup and saucer.

Limoges, Laviolette, c. 1896 – 1905.

Cup unusually puffed out at bottom, unusual handle; dainty hand-painted flowers, gold work.

$50.00 – 75.00.

Covered bouillon cup and saucer.

Limoges, GDA for Wright, Tyndale, & Van Roden, Philadelphia, c. 1900 – 1941.

Waisted, molded cup, slightly scalloped saucer and cover; mixed decoration on pale green.

$85.00 – 100.00.

Demitasse cup and saucer.

Limoges, Redon, c. 1891 – 1896.

Straight-sided cup, loop handle with molded dots; professional floral mixed decoration.

$35.00 – 45.00.

Demitasse cup and saucer.

Limoges, Bawo and Dotter, c. 1896 – 1900.

Unusual six-fluted and blown-out cup with ornate gilt handle; delicate floral decoration.

$65.00 – 75.00.

Chocolate cup and saucer.

Limoges, Lanternier, c. 1891 – 1914.

Slightly flared ribbed on bottom, scalloped saucer, rustic handle; professionally decorated floral.

$45.00 – 55.00.

Chocolate cup and saucer.

Limoges, Bawo and Dotter, c. 1920 – 1932.

Ribbed and molded cup with ornate gilt handle, scalloped saucer; delicate gold leafy decoration on pale pink.

$50.00 – 75.00.

Café-au-Lait cup and saucer.

Limoges, Bawo and Dotter, c. 1896 – 1900.

Lovely molded cup with unusual divided rustic handle, scalloped saucer; floral transfer.

$55.00 – 75.00.

Bouillon cup and saucer.

Limoges, D. & Co., decorated by Bernardaud & Co., c. 1900.

Round cup with ornate scrolled handles; beautiful hand-painted gilt florals. (See mark #59.)

$75.00 – 95.00.

Demitasse cup and saucer.

Limoges, Bawo & Dotter, c. 1896 – 1900.

Ribbed cup with rustic handle; professionally decorated gilt florals on coral, Japanese prunis motif.

$40.00 – 60.00.

Chocolate cup and saucer.

Limoges, Theodore Haviland, c. 1904 – 1925.

Fluted and molded cup and saucer, ear-shaped handle; floral and gilt decoration.

$40.00 – 55.00.

Demitasse cup and saucer.

Limoges, Haviland & Co., c. 1893 – 1930.

Straight-sided cup, scalloped saucer; delicate floral mixed decoration.

$40.00 – 50.00.

Teacup, saucer, and dessert plate.

Limoges, Haviland & Co., c. 1893 – 1930.

Slightly fluted round cup with kicked loop handle; scalloped saucer and plate; floral garlands.

$80.00 – 100.00.

Teacup and saucer.

Limoges, Theodore Haviland, c. 1903 – 1925.

Garland and bead mold cup with wide loop handle and scalloped saucer; delicate violets and daisies.

$35.00 – 45.00.

Demitasse cup and saucer.

Limoges, Theodor, Haviland, c. 1905 – 1925.

Low cup with narrow loop handle, scalloped saucer with gilt trim; pale pink flowers.

$40.00 – 50.00.

Demitasse cup and saucer.

Limoges, Haviland & Co., c. 1893 – 1930.

Molded cup with beaded loop handle, scalloped saucer; pastel flowers.

$40.00 – 50.00.

Same cup and saucer as above with different flowers.

Teacup and saucer.

Limoges, home decorated, c. 1890s.

Pedestal cup, broken loop handle with spurs; gold flowers, green leaves on white.

$45.00 – 60.00.

Demitasse cup and saucer.

Limoges, T. & V., c. 1892 – 1907.

Quatrefoil cup and saucer, wavy handle; hand-painted forget-me-nots on pale blue.

$45.00 – 60.00.

Coffee cup and saucer.

Limoges, probably home decorated, c. 1900.

Pedestal cup with high "D" handle; medallions of hand-painted musical instruments trimmed in gold.

$45.00 – 60.00.

Demitasse cup and saucer.

Limoges, Redon, M., c. 1896.

Swirled trefoil cup with broken loop handle; hand-painted cupid.

$60.00 – 80.00.

Chocolate cup and saucer.

Limoges, Pouyat, J., dated 1895.

Straight cup with loop handle; flower decorated.

$45.00 – 60.00.

Demitasse cup and saucer.

Limoges, c. 1891+.

Low cup with loop handle; home hand-painted decoration, gold flowers on yellow and white.

$35.00 – 45.00.

Teacup and saucer.

Limoges, Borgfeldt, c. 1906 – 1920.

Slightly waisted tapered cup with unusual angular rustic handle; rose decoration with dark green and coral.

$45.00 – 60.00.

Demitasse cup and saucer.

Limoges, Bawo & Dotter, c. 1896 – 1900.

Eight-fluted cup with slightly twisted loop handle; hand gilded flowers on pale yellow flower mold, light blue.

$75.00 – 100.00.

Teacup and saucer.

Limoges, Ahrenfeldt, C., c. 1894 – 1930s.

Low cup with loop handle; bands of red and gold with heavy gilt scrolls. (See mark #54.)

$45.00 – 60.00.

Demitasse cup and saucer.

Limoges, T. & V., c. 1892 – 1907.

Low cup with loop handle, heavy gold enameled leaves on cream.

$45.00 – 60.00.

Demitasse cup and saucer.

Limoges, Pouyat, J., made for Wright Tyndale & Van Roden, Philadelphia, c. 1914 – 1932.

Molded beading on rim of cup and saucer; roses and gilt leaf decoration.

$40.00 – 50.00.

Demitasse cup and saucer.

Limoges, Pouyat, Jean, c. 1891 – 1932.

Cup tapered in at bottom; loop handle; pale blue with gilt flowers.

$40.00 – 50.00.

Teacup and saucer.

Limoges, Haviland & Co., c. 1876 – 1889.

Bucket-shaped cup with circular rope handle; home decorated with butterfly and pink flowers.

$50.00 – 60.00.

Same cup and saucer as above with different decorations.

Teacup and saucer.

Limoges, Haviland & Co., c. 1876 – 1930.

Cup with molded border, scalloped saucer, and rustic handle; pink flowers.

$40.00 – 50.00.

Teacup and saucer.

Limoges, T. & V., dated 1922.

Footed and 12-paneled at waist, square handle; colorful Art Deco band with hand-painted oranges on gold.

$40.00 – 50.00.

Demitasse cup and saucer.

Limoges, Demartine, c. 1891 – 1900.

Ten-paneled cup with rustic handle, unusual scalloped saucer; white roses.

$45.00 – 55.00.

Teacup and saucer.

Limoges, Bawo & Dotter, c. 1900 – 1914.

Slightly tapered cup with loop handle; hand-painted Art Nouveau leaf decoration.

$60.00 – 85.00.

Teacup and saucer.

Limoges, GDA, c. 1900 – 1941.

Molded cup with loop handle, delicate floral transfer. (See mark #60.)

$40.00 – 50.00.

Demitasse cup and saucer.

Limoges, T. & V., home decorated, initials G. H., c. 1892 – 1907.

Low cup with loop handle; pearlized band of gold flowers and bars on green.

$30.00 – 40.00.

Demitasse cup and saucer.

Limoges, Bernardaud & Co., c. 1900 – 1930.

Molded cross hatch motif on cup and saucer, ornate handle; hand-painted monochrome painting of lake scene.

$60.00 – 75.00.

Teacup and saucer.

Limoges, Haviland & Co. for the Amstel, c. 1910 – 1924.

Short cup (only 2" high) with angular loop handle with gilt dots and feathers; lovely rose transfer.

$45.00 – 60.00.

Teacup and saucer.

Limoges, Haviland, home decorated, signed and dated 1894.

Rare left-handed cup with ornate broken loop handle; lovely hand-painted floral design.

$75.00 – 95.00.

Teacup and saucer.

Limoges, Union Ceramique, made for Marshall Field & Co., c. 1909 – 1939.

Round cup; transfer of children playing.

$35.00 – 50.00.

Demitasse cup and saucer.

Limoges, GDA, c. 1900 – 1941.

Slightly ribbed and tapered cup with loop handle with inner spurs; delicate floral decoration.

$35.00 – 45.00.

Teacup and saucer.

Limoges, Haviland & Co., c. 1888 – 1896.

Straight-sided molded cup, deep saucer; delicate hand-painted flowers. (See mark #66.)

$40.00 – 55.00.

Teacup and saucer.

Limoges, Haviland, Theodore, c. 1893.

Waisted cup with ear-shaped handle; translucent white porcelain with gold waves. (See mark #67.)

$30.00 – 40.00.

Chocolate cup and saucer.

Limoges, Pouyat, J., c. 1914 – 1932.

Slightly flared cup with unusual double loop handle; band of green leaves. (See mark #72.)

$30.00 – 40.00.

Snack set.

Limoges, GDM, c. 1882 – 1890.

Cup with fan handle; heavy saucer with ribbing on rim, molded indentation for cup; transfer of forget-me-nots. (See mark #61.)

$125.00 – 150.00.

Same as above with different pattern.

Teacup and saucer.

Limoges, Haviland, c. 1893 – 1930.

Tapered cup, scalloped saucer, gold ribbon handle; mixed floral decoration.

$40.00 – 50.00.

Snack set.

Haviland & Co., c. 1876 – 1930.

Footed cup with loop handle, scalloped tray in an uneven shape; tiny blue floral decoration.

$100.00 – 125.00.

Demitasse cup and saucer.

Limoges, Coiffe with fake Sevres mark, c. 1891 – 1914.

Straight cup with scalloped saucer; lovely hand gilded scrolls on dark red.

$75.00 – 95.00.

Snack set.

Limoges, T. & V., home decorated, R. Mills, c. 1892 – 1907.

Rounded cup with wonderful ornate handle; Art Nouveau Persian decoration.

$150.00 – 175.00.

Snack set.

Limoges, T. & V., home decorated, R. Mills, c. 1892 – 1907.

Same form as above; 24 karat gold Art Nouveau decoration.

$150.00 – 175.00.

Snack set.

Limoges, T. & V., home decorated, A. Miller, c. 1892 – 1907.

Same form as above; sea gull decoration.

$150.00 – 175.00.

Teacup and saucer.

Limoges, Redon, M., c. 1882 – 1896.

Low round cup with loop handle; ½" gold band on rim of cup and saucer; floral transfer. (See mark #73.)

$45.00 – 60.00.

Teacup and saucer.

Limoges, Guerin, c. 1900 – 1932.

Bucket-shaped cup with angular handle; two etched ½" bands on cup and saucer; floral transfer. (See mark #63.)

$45.00 – 60.00.

Teacup, saucer, and dessert plate.

Limoges, Bawo & Dotter, c. 1920 – 1932.

Bucket-shaped cup with reinforced loop handle; delicate flowers on coral shaded to white ground. (See mark #56.)

$75.00 – 95.00.

Teacup and saucer.

HenRiot Quimper, c. 1920s.

Bucket-shaped cup with square handle; hand-painted medallion of boy playing flute.

$150.00 – 200.00.

Teacup and saucer.

"Sevres" mark, c. 1890s.

Twelve-paneled footed cup with square handle; medallions of hand-painted flowers, hand gilded on blue.

$100.00 – 125.00.

Demitasse cup and saucer.

"Sevres" mark, c. 1890s.

Pedestal cup with ornate gilt handle; garlands of hand-painted roses, gilt work, maroon and pink.

$125.00 – 150.00.

Teacup and saucer.

Belleek Pottery Company, 1965 – 1980.

Cup in Harp Shamrock body shape.

$60.00 – 75.00.

Demitasse cup and saucer.

Belleek Pottery Company, c. 1926 – 1946.

Limpet form.

$100.00 – 125.00.

Teacup, saucer, and dessert plate.

Belleek Pottery Company, c. 1955 – 1965.

Shamrock form.

$100.00 – 125.00.

Snack set.

Belleek Pottery Company, c. 1955 – 1965.

Shamrock form.

$115.00 – 130.00.

Teacup and saucer.

Belleek Pottery Company, c. 1955 – 1965.

Shell form.

$60.00 – 75.00.

Demitasse cup and saucer.

Belleek Pottery Company, c. 1965 – 1980.

Shamrock form.

$50.00 – 60.00.

Snack set.

Belleek Pottery Company, c. 1965 – 1980.

Tridacna form.

$115.00 – 130.00.

Demitasse cup and saucer.

Castleton China, Inc., c. 1940+.

Waisted footed cup with broken loop handle; Sovereign.

$35.00 – 45.00.

Demitasse cup and saucer.

Cemar, California, c. 1946 – 1957.

Figural cup of strawberry, leaf-shaped saucer.

$40.00 – 50.00.

Teacup and saucer.

Knowles, Taylor & Knowles, E. Liverpool, Ohio, c. 1925.

Low, slightly flared cup with loop handle; band with floral transfer.

$25.00 – 35.00.

Teacup and saucer.

Lefton China, c. 1949 – 1955.

Pedestal cup with reinforced broken loop handle; large black band with gold stars, rose transfer inside cup and in well of saucer. (See mark #53.)

$40.00 – 50.00.

Teacup and saucer.

Lefton China, c. 1949 – 1955.

Footed cup with molded hearts, square handle; purple flowers inside recessed hearts.

$30.00 – 40.00.

Teacup and saucer.

Lefton China, c. 1949 – 1955.

Three-footed fluted cup, reticulated saucer; blue pearl luster, round gold designs.

$35.00 – 45.00.

Teacup and saucer.

Leneige China, Burbank, California, c. 1952.

Corset-shaped cup with loop handle; black with pink inside cup, gilded branches and leaves.

$30.00 – 40.00.

Demitasse cup and saucer.

Lenox, c. 1950s.

Footed cup with French Loop Handle; Colonial.

$40.00 – 50.00.

Teacup and saucer.

Lenox, c. 1920s.

Six-sided cup and saucer, angular handle, cream and gold.

$50.00 – 65.00.

Demitasse cup and saucer.

Lenox, c. 1930s.

Bute cup with loop handle; Pembroke.

$50.00 – 65.00.

Demitasse cup and saucer.

Lenox, c. 1950s.

Footed and 24-ribbed cup and saucer, square handle; enameled floral design.

$40.00 – 50.00.

Demitasse cup and saucer.

Lenox, c. 1920s.

Tridacna form in pink.

$50.00 – 65.00.

Demitasse cup and saucer.

Lenox, c. 1930.

Bute cup with loop handle; bird transfer with gold band on cream.

$40.00 – 50.00.

Demitasse cup and saucer.

Lenox, c. 1950s.

Bute cup with loop handle; Cattail.

$40.00 – 50.00.

Teacup and saucer.

Pickard on Nippon blank, c. 1895 – 1898.

Low cup with loop handle; band on gold with scattered flowers.

$100.00 – 125.00.

Demitasse cup and saucer.

Scanmel China Co., Trenton, New Jersey, c. 1926 – 1954.

Straight-sided cup with ring handle; parrot and flowers.

$30.00 – 40.00.

Demitasse cup and saucer.

Stouffer Co., c. 1938 – 1946.

Bucket-shaped cup with foot rim; ornate handle; "Golden Orchid"; artist signed.

$50.00 – 60.00.

Demitasse cup and saucer.

Syracuse China, c. 1930s.

Cup ribbed at bottom, crimped saucer; Shelledge pattern.

$30.00 – 35.00.

Demitasse cup and saucer.

Van Briggle, c. 1950s.

Straight cup with question mark handle; turquoise glaze. (See mark #115.)

$60.00 – 90.00.

Demitasse cup and saucer.

Vernon Kilns, made in USA, c. 1931+.

Tapered cup with upside-down loop handle; Hawaiian Flowers, designed by Aloha Don Blandig.

$50.00 – 60.00.

Demitasse cup and saucer.

Willets Manufacturing Company, c. 1885 – 1909.

Cup on square pedestal base, angular handle; silver deposit decoration on Belleek body.

$100.00 – 125.00.

Teacup and saucer.

Japanese Imari, c. 1900 – 1920.

Paneled cup and saucer with different design in each panel. (See mark #50.)

$75.00 – 100.00.

Teacup and saucer.

Nippon, c. 1891 – 1921.

Six-sided cup with loop handle; medallions of hand-painted peonies, gold checkerboard motif.

$80.00 – 100.00.

Teacup and saucer.

Nippon, green "M" in wreath, Noritake, c. 1891 – 1921.

Pedestal cup with wonderful handle; hand-painted flowers with beaded rim.

$65.00 – 75.00.

Demitasse cup and saucer.

Unmarked, probably pre-Nippon, c. 1880s.

Molded, very thin porcelain cup with thick loop handle; hand-painted floral medallions on cobalt.

$50.00 – 75.00.

Teacup and saucer.

Noritake, c. 1940s.

Rounded cup with loop handle; Dresden style flowers.

$30.00 – 35.00.

Teacup and saucer.

Royal Sealy, Japan, c. 1950s+.

Footed cup, loop handle with thumb rest and inner spur; gilded fruit design much like those made by Aynsley.

$35.00 – 45.00.

Teacup and saucer.

Royal Sealy, Japan, c. 1950+.

Melon-shaped cup on three gold feet; gold floral decoration on turquoise.

$35.00 – 40.00.

Teacup and saucer.

Unmarked, probably Japanese, c. 1880s.

Unusual cup with fish handle; hand gilded scrollwork on aqua, shaded to yellow.

$60.00 – 80.00.

Small demitasse cup and saucer.

Unmarked, except #19, probably Japan, c. 1900.

Scalloped cup with loop handle, leaf-shaped saucer; Victoria and Albert commemorative.

$40.00 – 60.00.

Teacup and saucer.

Crossed flags mark, Japan, c. 1920s.

Swirled cup and saucer, gilt loop handle with thumb rest; delicate moriage decoration; heavily enameled flowers.

$40.00 – 50.00.

Teacup and saucer.

Unmarked, Japanese, possibly pre-Nippon.

Twelve-fluted, three-footed cup with loop handle; cobalt blue, hand-painted flower medallions.

$70.00 – 90.00.

Demitasse cup and saucer.

Unmarked, Japan, c. 1930 – 1950s.

Straight-sided lithophane with loop handle; Blue Willow.

$40.00 – 50.00.

Demitasse cup and saucer.

Japanese, unidentified cartouche, c. 1930s.

Puffy cup on foot rim, loop handle with sharp inner spur, lithophane; trees and flowers with gilt overpainting.

$40.00 – 50.00.

View of lithophane inside above cup.

Demitasse cup and saucer.

Japanese marks, c. 1930s.

Delicate rounded cup on gold banded foot, loop handle with inner spur; floral design, Japanese lady lithophane.

$40.00 – 50.00.

Teacup and saucer.

Unmarked Japan, c. 1930s.

Rounded cup with loop handle, lithophane; moriage dragon motif.

$25.00 – 40.00.

Demitasse cup and saucer.

Unmarked, Japanese, c. 1920 – 30s.

Swirled, thin-walled cup with ring handle; hand gilded flowers.

$25.00 – 35.00.

Pot de creme and saucer.

Unidentified mark with peacock.

Rounded cup with angular handle; flower and leaf decoration.

$40.00 – 60.00.

ENGLISH TABLEWARES

Many English companies have produced beautiful teacups and saucers. During the early twentieth century, lovely bone china and earthenware dinnerware with colorful transfer or hand-painted decoration were produced. Many sets were exported to the United States and Canada, and it became fashionable for young brides to collect sample cups and saucers from different sets. Today these single sets of English teacups and saucers are still eagerly collected. They are not just displayed in a china cabinet, however; they are used, especially at dinner parties and teas, where each guest can select his or her own unique teacup and saucer.

ADAMS

William Adams & Sons began operation in 1769 and is one of the oldest names in the Staffordshire Pottery industry. Adams was a favorite pupil of Josiah Wedgwood and made jasperware to rival Wedgwood's. Beginning in 1905 and up to the 1950s, Adams made a line of hand-painted earthenware on ivory ground with flowers and fruits in bold bright colors. This Art Deco line was called Titian Ware and has begun to attract the attention of collectors. Titian Ware looks very much like the Czechoslovakian peasant designs of the period. A line was also produced by S. Hancock & Sons in the 1920s.

ADDERLEYS COMPANY

The Adderleys Company first began its life at Daisy Bank Pottery in Longton, Stoke-on-Trent, named because it was said to have been built on a bank of daisies. It was originally one of the factories belonging to the Mason pottery family, but in 1852 it was taken over by a partnership composed of three men, including Rupert Adderley. After a few changes, the company was renamed Wm. A. Adderley & Co., in 1886. In 1895 William Adderley retired from the company, but it retained the Adderley name, becoming Adderleys Ltd., in 1905. In 1973 the company became part of the Royal Doulton Company, which today continues to own the Adderleys name. Adderley Floral China, now renamed Royal Adderley, is a branch of Ridgway Potteries, Ltd., that is also part of the Royal Doulton group. During the last 30 years, Royal Adderley has become known for their lovely life-like bone china birds, applied flower arrangements, and bone china dinnerware.

AYNSLEY CHINA

A popular name in twentieth century tableware is Aynsley China. Geoffrey Goddens says, "Aynsley is one of the leading fine bone china firms of this present century. Their ware is above average, and some of it is superb."

John Aynsley established a pottery in 1775 in Longton, and as tea drinking became more and more fashionable in England, he turned to tea and dessert services. By the turn of the nineteenth century, he was making them of bone china, still the present company's specialty. His aim, carried on today, was to produce a superior type of body, pure in tone but sound and durable, in shapes that were useful and artistic.

Aynsley has received royal patronage many times in the twentieth century. Queen Elizabeth selected an Aynsley service at the time of her wedding, and this was continued by the late Princess Diana. In 1969 Aynsley joined with Waterford Crystal. Today Aynsley operates four factories within the Stoke-on-Trent area.

Pembroke, originally produced more than 100 years ago, Leighton Cobalt, and the Wild Tudor patterns are popular in the United States. The beautiful "Fruit" cups in the Oban and Athens shapes are eagerly collected today. The fruit patterns were designed by Doris Jones, an

Cooper designed the popular Contemporary Style shapes and patterns.

ROYAL CROWN DERBY

Royal Crown Derby continues to produce beautiful dinnerware of exceptional quality. The production of their famous Japanese patterns, or Imari, was greatly increased in the late nineteenth century. Patterns currently in production are #383, #1128, and the always popular #2451. Many copies have been made of the Derby Japans, often with inferior gold and a lack of workmanship.

CROWN STAFFORDSHIRE

The Crown Staffordshire Porcelain Company was established in 1833 by Thomas Green and remained in the Green family until 1964. It is now part of the Wedgwood Group. The company originally made earthenware decorated in the Chinese style with flowers and transferware printed in blue, black, brown, green, and pink. They specialized in the reproduction of old English pottery and early Chinese forms and colors.

The pottery claimed to be the most successful producers of old Chinese "powder blue" and rose colors as the result of extensive testing.

During the 1950s a wide range of bone china tableware patterns and giftware utilizing modern and traditional designs was produced. Miniature tea sets with trays, which were exact replicas of full-size productions, were also made and are collected today by miniature enthusiasts. Chief designer David Queensberry designed special tableware patterns and a famous set of nurseryware, and these are marked with his name.

ROYAL DOULTON

The Doulton Company created some of the most beautiful dinnerware services in their Burslem factory in the late nineteenth century. They continued to make many stylish bone china tablewares as well as their popular line of Series Wares in the 1920s and 1930s. These were standard bone china or pottery items, such as plates, jugs, and teaware, decorated with hand-colored transfer prints of popular themes. Examples were games, characters from legends and stories, hunting scenes, and children. They were sold as novelty wares to the general public, and bring high prices today.

FOLEY CHINA WORKS

Foley China Works (E. Brain & Co., Ltd.) was established in Fenton, c. 1903 – 1963. Since 1963 production has continued under the Coalport name. The tradition of using well-known designers and artists was established at the Foley Company in the 1930s where they commissioned people such as Graham Sutherland, Maureen Tanner, and Paul Nash to create designs for them.

HAMMERSLEY & CO.

Hammersley & Co. was established in Longton in 1887 and is still in operation today. The company produced an excellent quality of bone china tablewares. A pattern with bold roses and gilding was popular through the 1920s. Hammersley tea ware resembles the richly gilded and bright colored examples made by Aynsley and Paragon.

GEORGE JONES

George Jones, a former Minton employee, founded his firm at the Old Bridge Works, Stoke-on-Trent, in 1861. Soon after, Jones became a successful maker of fine quality majolica, art pottery, and bone china. His fine tablewares are beginning to be appreciated by collectors.

MINTON

Since it began operation in 1793, Minton

has produced fine porcelains, often with magnificent gilding and hand painting. After World War II the Minton Company's high quality bone china tableware was in considerable demand at home and abroad. Many new patterns were designed, including the best selling Haddon Hall pattern, first designed in 1949. Old patterns were still popular, especially Minton Rose, introduced in 1854. In 1968 Minton became part of the Royal Doulton Tableware Group. Many cups with beautiful ring and butterfly handles are still being produced.

PARAGON CHINA

Paragon China was established in Longton in 1920. The company was taken over by T. C. Wild & Sons, Ltd. in 1960 and is now part of the Royal Doulton Tableware Group. From its beginning, Paragon became known for its fine bone china, specializing in breakfast, tea, and dessert ware. Much was exported to the United States and Canada. The company has received royal patronage and support, and this is reflected in their trademarks. Collectors look for the richly gilded cups and saucers with bold flowers and dramatic ground colors.

ROYAL ALBERT

Royal Albert was established by Thomas C. Wild in 1896 in Longton, and is now part of the Royal Doulton Tableware Group. Royal Albert produced a tremendous output of bone china tablewares, and much has been exported to the United States and Canada. Popular patterns are Moss Rose, Heirloom, and Royalty. Old Country Roses was designed by Harold Holdcroft in 1962 and is one of the most popular dinnerware patterns of all time. In the 1950s Royal Albert produced the "Flower of the Month" cup and saucer series that is eagerly collected today.

SHELLEY

Shelley bone china dinnerware is admired by royalty, statesmen, and thousands of brides the world over. In 1872 Joseph Shelley became partners with James Wileman, owner of Foley China Works, thus creating Wileman & Company in Stoke-on-Trent. Wileman later withdrew, and in 1825 the company became known as Shelley Potteries, Ltd. It was taken over by Allied English Potteries in 1966 and is now part of the Royal Doulton Tableware Group.

Percy Shelley hired various well-known artists and designers. Rowland Morris, who apprenticed at Minton, designed the "Dainty" shape in 1896, and it became the most popular and successful shape in Shelley's history. Many floral designs were produced in the "Dainty" shape, such as Dainty Blue and Dainty Pink. The Regency pattern, which is the "Dainty" shape in white with gold trim on the edges and handles, is very popular.

During the 1920s many styles of cups and saucers were made, some having from six to 16 flutes. The porcelain was so delicate it was referred to as the "eggshell china" and established Shelley's reputation as a leading producer of quality dinnerware services. The many popular patterns were decorated with lovely pastel floral transfers.

Another outstanding shape, "Queen Anne," was designed in 1926. Over 170 floral patterns and garden scenes were applied to this shape. During the Art Deco period the "Vogue" shape was introduced. It was popular, but some objected to the highly tapered shape, complaining that tea and coffee cooled too rapidly in it. In response Shelley developed "Mode" which was less tapered. This shape was also criticized because the handle was solid, preventing the user from putting a finger in the opening or hanging the cup from a hook. A new shape, "Eve," was developed, combining the best features of "Vogue" and "Mode."

TORQUAY

Torquay pottery got its name from the Torquay district in South Devon, England. The most well-known company producing this popular pottery is Watcombe Pottery, who started making terra cotta "Motto ware" in 1870. The designs were painted in thick colored slip and finished with a clear glaze. Rhymes or proverbs

Demitasse cup and saucer.

Adams Titian Ware, c. 1896 – 1920s.

Slightly tapered cup, loop handle with spur; hand-painted flowers.

$30.00 – 35.00.

Teacup and saucer.

Adams Titian Ware, c. 1896 – 1920s.

Round cup with loop handle; hand-painted flowers and cobalt blue band.

$30.00 – 35.00.

Teacup and saucer.

Adams Titian Ware, c. 1896 – 1920s.

Slightly flared cup, ring handle; hand-painted leaves with cut sponge flowers and berries.

$30.00 – 40.00.

Demitasse cup and saucer.

Adams Titian Ware, c. 1896 – 1920s.

Pedestal cup with loop handle; "Della Monte" border, cream.

$20.00 – 25.00.

Teacup and saucer.

Adams Titian Ware, c. 1896 – 1920s.

Round cup, ring handle with thumb rest; Wynbrook pattern.

$30.00 – 35.00.

Teacup and saucer.

Adams Titian Ware, c. 1896 – 1920s.

Flared footed cup with loop handle; "Della Robia" border; hand-painted design.

$30.00 – 35.00.

Demitasse cup and saucer.

Adams Titian Ware, c. 1896 – 1920s.

Flared footed cup with loop handle, "Della Robbia" border, hand-painted design.

$30.00 – 35.00.

Teacup and saucer.

Adams Titian Ware, c. 1896 – 1920s.

Round cup with loop handle; hand-painted fruits.

$30.00 – 35.00.

Bouillon cup and saucer.

Adams Titian Ware, c. 1896 – 1920s.

Pedestal cup with two loop handles with thumb rests; Faenza pattern and "Della Monte" border.

$30.00 – 35.00.

Teacup and saucer.

Adderleys Ltd., c. 1962+.

Footed and waisted cup with curled, kicked loop handle; Lawley pattern.

$30.00 – 40.00.

Teacup and saucer.

Adderleys Ltd., c. 1962 – present.

Footed cup with pinched, kicked loop handle; delicate purple flowers.

$30.00 – 35.00.

Teacup and saucer.

Adderleys, Ltd. c. 1962.

Twelve-fluted cup and saucer; yellow ground with violets inside cup. (See mark #2.)

$40.00 – 45.00.

Teacup and saucer.

Aynsley, John & Sons, c. 1950s.

Low Doris shape; bands of dark red and pale yellow; hand-gilded leafy design, floral transfer in center. (See mark #7.)

$40.00 – 55.00.

Teacup and saucer.

Aynsley, c. 1950s.

Low Doris shape; gilt leafy design on bands of turquoise and white.

$30.00 – 45.00.

Teacup and saucer.

Aynsley, c. 1950s.

Corset-shaped cup with coiled loop handle; gold leafy design on turquoise.

$30.00 – 45.00.

Teacup and saucer.

Aynsley, c. 1950s.

Athens shape; gold scrolled decoration and band of turquoise.

$35.00 – 50.00.

Teacup and saucer.

Aynsley, c. 1950s.

York shape; dark red and gold flowers.

$35.00 – 45.00.

Teacup and saucer.

Aynsley, c. 1950s.

York shape; yellow with gold flowers on rim.

$30.00 – 40.00.

Teacup and saucer.

Aynsley, c. 1950s.

Corset-shaped cup with coiled handle; pale green with leafy design.

$30.00 – 40.00.

Snack set.

Aynsley, c. 1891 – 1920.

Slightly scalloped with "D" shaped handle; colorful row of flowers.

$35.00 – 45.00.

Teacup and saucer.

Aynsley, c. 1950s.

Athens shape; orange rim with gold leaf design; rose inside cup.

$40.00 – 55.00.

Teacup, saucer, and plate.

Aynsley, c. 1891 – 1920.

Low Doris shape; lovely garlands and baskets of roses on white, band of pink.

$75.00 – 100.00.

Teacup and saucer.

Aynsley, c. 1950s.

Footed, scalloped, and leaf-molded cup with ornate handle with thumb rest; scenic transfer on pale blue.

$40.00 – 55.00.

Teacup and saucer.

Aynsley, c. 1950 – present.

Low Doris shape; pink and white flower transfer on pale peach inside cup and on saucer.

$35.00 – 45.00.

Teacup and saucer.

Aynsley, c. 1950s – present.

Corset-shaped cup with coiled handle; turquoise, white, and gilt decoration.

$35.00 – 45.00.

Teacup and saucer.

Aynsley, c. 1930s.

Athens shape; "double fruit," signed D. Jones. (See mark #6.)

$125.00 – 150.00.

Close-up of saucer above.

Teacup and saucer.

Aynsley, c. 1950s.

Footed cup with feathered, coiled loop handle; turquoise with fruit; gilt.

$80.00 – 100.00.

Teacup and saucer.

Aynsley, c. 1930s.

Oban shape, fruit inside, cobalt ground, signed D. Jones.

$115.00 – 135.00.

Teacup and saucer.

Aynsley, c. 1930s.

Athens shape; fruit inside cup, green ground, signed D. Jones.

$100.00 – 125.00.

Teacup and saucer.

Aynsley, c. 1950s.

Cup with ornate gilded handle and foot; magnificent butterfly design inside cup, cobalt blue.

$125.00 – 150.00.

Teacup and saucer.

Aynsley, c. 1950s.

Footed, fluted cup, scalloped saucer; bright peony and other flowers transfer.

$40.00 – 50.00.

Snack set.

Aynsley, c. 1891 – 1920.

Slightly scalloped cup and saucer with "D" handle; bright yellow band with black design.

$30.00 – 40.00.

Teacup and saucer.

Aynsley, c. 1950s.

Athens shape, gilt inside cup; beautiful roses.

$90.00 – 125.00.

Teacup and saucer.

Aynsley, c. 1950s.

Athens shape; rare ship design inside cup, red ground.

$100.00 – 125.00.

Teacup and saucer.

Aynsley, c. 1920s.

Slightly scalloped cup with "D" handle; Queens Garden. (See mark #5.)

$35.00 – 50.00.

Teacup and saucer.

Aynsley, c. 1930s.

Slightly flared cup with fat loop handle; Imari pattern.

$50.00 – 75.00.

Teacup and saucer.

Booths Ltd., c. 1912+.

Low-waisted, footed cup with squared handle; Blue Willow pattern with lovely gilt decoration.

$40.00 – 50.00.

Teacup and saucer.

Booths Ltd., c. 1915 – 1925.

Cup with London shape, scalloped saucer; Chinese Tree pattern.

$35.00 – 45.00.

Teacup and saucer.

Booths Ltd., c. 1915 – 1925.

London style cup with scalloped saucer; gilt edge on cup and saucer; Dragon pattern.

$35.00 – 45.00.

Demitasse cups and saucers.

Brown-Westhead, Moore & Co., made for the George Ford Co., New Haven, Connecticut, c. 1890 – 1895.

Scalloped cups with ruffled feet, divided stem handles; aqua to white, to pink, and pink shaded to white to yellow, garlands of small roses. (See mark #11.)

$50.00 – 60.00 each.

Teacup.

Carlton Ware, c. 1970s.

Walking Wear novelty pattern, green shoes with purple stars on socks.

$75.00 – 100.00.

Demitasse cup and saucer.

Cauldon Ltd., c. 1905 – 1920, made for Tiffany & Co., New York.

Straight cup with gilt loop handle; gold floral and geometric design on ivory, cobalt band with hand-decorated gilt.

$50.00 – 75.00.

Teacup and saucer.

Cauldon Potteries Ltd., c. 1950 – 1962.

Waisted and scalloped pedestal cup, slightly scalloped saucer; multicolored floral transfer.

$30.00 – 40.00.

Teacup, saucer, and plate.

Cauldon Ltd., c. 1905 – 1920.

Earthenware cup in London shape; colorful Oriental bird design. (See mark #14.)

$60.00 – 75.00.

Teacup and saucer.

Clare China Co. Ltd., c. 1951 – present.

Slightly waisted and footed cup with "question mark" handle; gilt floral pattern around large pink rose.

$35.00 – 45.00.

Teacup and saucer.

Clarence Bone China (Cooperative Wholesale Society Ltd.), c. 1960s.

Footed quatrefoil cup with broken loop handle; fruit transfer.

$30.00 – 35.00.

Teacup and saucer.

Coalport, c. 1891 – 1919.

Slightly scalloped pedestal cup and saucer; attractive cobalt and gold loop handle with spurs; pink roses, cobalt spokes.

$50.00 – 75.00.

Teacup, saucer, and dessert plate.

Coalport, c. 1950s.

Scalloped cup and saucer, loop handle with feathered thumb rest; Hazelton.

$100.00 – 125.00.

Teacup and saucer.

Coalport, c. 1945 – 1959.

Scalloped and pedestal cup, loop handle with prominent spurs; Cairo.

$40.00 – 50.00.

Teacup and saucer.

Coalport, c. 1945 – 1959.

Pedestal, scalloped cup and saucer; Cairo pattern.

$40.00 – 50.00.

Small teacup and saucer.

Coalport, c. 1891 – 1920.

Unusual ten-sided cup and saucer with raised well; Indian Tree pattern.

$45.00 – 60.00.

Snack set.

Coalport, c. 1891 – 1919.

Eight dainty flutes with unusual loop handle; Flower Pots.

$50.00 – 75.00.

Snack set.

Coalport, c. 1890 – 1925.

Round cup, small tray, "C" shaped handle with thumb rest; floral with green band.

$50.00 – 75.00.

Demitasse cup and saucer.

Royal Crown Derby, c. 1891.

Bute cup with loop handle; cobalt blue and white; Osborne pattern. (See mark #26.)

$40.00 – 50.00.

Teacup and saucer. (closeup)

Royal Crown Derby, c. 1971.

Footed, slightly flared cup, reinforced loop handle; Imari pattern #1128. (See mark #28.)

$85.00 – 100.00.

Teacup and saucer.

Royal Crown Derby, c. 1971.

Footed, slightly flared cup, reinforced loop handle; Imari pattern #1128. (See mark #28.)

$85.00 – 100.00.

Teacup, saucer, and dessert plate.

Royal Crown Derby, c. 1950s.

Flared cup with pinched loop handle with feathered thumb rest; Derby Posies pattern.

$100.00 – 125.00.

Teacup and saucer.

Royal Crown Derby, c. 1969.

Chelsea shape cup; gilt Olde Avesbury pattern.

$50.00 – 75.00.

Teacup and saucer.

Crown Staffordshire, c. 1930s.

Footed cup with blue squarish handle; floral transfer. (See mark #23.)

$35.00 – 45.00.

Demitasse cup and saucer.

Crown Staffordshire, c. 1960s.

Can with loop handle; royal Commemorative. (See mark #24.)

$35.00 – 45.00.

Demitasse cup and saucer.

Crown Staffordshire, c. 1930s.

Can with loop handle; chintz pattern.

$35.00 – 45.00.

Snack set.

Crown Staffordshire, c. 1930s+.

Waisted ribbed cup with broken loop handle; yellow daisies on white.

$30.00 – 40.00.

Teacup and saucer.

Crown Staffordshire, c. 1930 – present.

Paneled cup on bottom, unusual flower-shaped handle; Nasturtium.

$100.00 – 125.00.

Teacup and saucer.

Crown Staffordshire, c. 1950s.

Footed cup with square handle; Chinese Willow.

$40.00 – 50.00.

Demitasse cup and saucer.

Dartmouth Pottery Co., c. 1947 – present.

Round cup with loop handle; Motto Ware with cottage scene, inscribed 'Tis Very Refreshin', crazed.

$35.00 – 45.00.

Breakfast cup and saucer.

Doulton Burslem, c. 1882 – 1890.

Straight-sided cup with ring handle; floral transfer.

$80.00 – 100.00.

Teacup and saucer.

Duchess Bone China (A. T. Finney & Sons), c. 1947 – 1960.

Pear-shaped cup with loop handle; vivid florals.

$25.00 – 35.00.

Teacup and saucer.

Duchess Bone China, c. 1947 – 1960.

Scalloped, tapered, and waisted cup, scalloped saucer, loop handle with thumb rest; souvenir, "Atlantic Canada Coastal Scene."

$30.00 – 35.00.

Demitasse cups and saucers.

Elizabethan Fine Bone China, made exclusively for Tiffany & Co., c. 1964 – present.

Cans with reinforced loop handles; playing card motif. (See mark #37.)

$35.00 – 50.00 each.

Coffee cup and saucer.

Elizabethan Fine Bone China, c. 1964 – present.

Ribbed can with ornate broken loop handle; deck of cards motif.

$35.00 – 45.00.

Breakfast cup and saucer.

Elizabethan Fine Bone China, c. 1964 – present.

Footed cup with loop handle; Rolls Royce car on cup.

$25.00 – 40.00.

Teacup and saucer.

Foley Bone China (E. Brain & Co. Ltd.), c. 1948 – 1963.

Scalloped and flared cup, kicked loop handle with flat thumb rest; aqua with gilt leafy trim on rim; colorful bird transfer in center. (See mark #40.)

$40.00 – 55.00.

Teacup and saucer.

Foley, c. 1930 – 1935.

Waisted cup with loop handle; floral transfer. (See mark #38.)

$25.00 – 40.00.

Teacup and saucer.

Foley Bone China, c. 1953.

Scalloped cup with feathered loop handle; coronation of Queen Elizabeth. (See mark #39.)

$45.00 – 55.00.

Teacup and saucer.

Foley, c. 1930+.

Slightly flared cup with angular handle; hand-painted accents on transfer.

$35.00 – 45.00.

Teacup and saucer.

Foley, c. 1945 – 1963.

Pedestal cup with coiled loop handle; Cornflower.

$35.00 – 45.00.

Demitasse cup and saucer.

Foley, Peacock Pottery, c. 1905 – 1912.

Straight-sided cup with loop handle.

$40.00 – 50.00.

Teacup and saucer.

Foley, c. 1930 – present.

Slightly scalloped cup and saucer, backwards "C"-type handle; hand-painted accents on floral transfer.

$40.00 – 50.00.

Teacup and saucer.

Forester, Thomas & Sons Ltd., c. 1912 – 1959.

Tapered cup with loop handle; Oriental scene with dragon and Phoenix bird, gold leafing.

$40.00 – 55.00.

Teacup and saucer.

Grosvenor Fine Bone China (Jackson & Gosling), c. 1880s.

Flared, scalloped, waisted cup with "D" handle; hand-painted purple and gold floral design.

$40.00 – 50.00.

Teacup and saucer.

Grosvenor China Ltd., c. 1950 – 1961.

Scalloped, waisted, pedestal cup with loop handle with thumb rest; wide light-green band with scattered flowers, yellow foot and handle.

$25.00 – 40.00.

Teacup and saucer.

Hammersley & Co., c. 1939 – 1950s.

Footed, slightly fluted, and scalloped cup with ornate broken loop handle; Oriental pattern.

$50.00 – 60.00.

Teacup and saucer.

Hammersley & Co., c. 1939 – 1950s.

Footed, slightly fluted, and scalloped cup with ornate handle; lovely gold floral scrollwork on dark red. (See mark #43.)

$60.00 – 75.00.

Teacup and saucer.

Hammersley & Co., c. 1939 – 1952.

Slightly flared, scalloped cup; flowers in center and well; maroon band.

$35.00 – 45.00.

Teacup and saucer.

Hammersley, c. 1939 – 1950s.

Footed, scalloped, and waisted cup with broken loop handle with thumb rest; daffodils.

$35.00 – 45.00.

Demitasse cup and saucer.

Hudson and Middleton Ltd., Staffordshire, c. 1950 – present.

Can with loop handle; dark red and white with gold leafy trim.

$25.00 – 35.00.

Teacup and saucer.

George Jones, c. 1890.

Royal flute-shaped cup, scalloped saucer; lovely hand-painted flowers and heavy gilt leafy decoration. (See mark #51.)

$75.00 – 95.00.

Demitasse cup and saucer.

George Jones & Sons, c. 1891 – 1924.

Creamware tapered cup; loop handle with feathered thumb rest; Shannon.

$30.00 – 40.00.

Demitasse cup and saucer.

George Jones for Gilman & Collamore, c. 1891 – 1924.

Bute cup with loop handle; three blue bands with flowers scattered along it, blue beading.

$35.00 – 50.00.

Teacup and saucer.

James Kent, Ltd., c. 1934 – 1980.

Royal Flute shape with broken loop handle; chintz, DuBarry.

$90.00 – 115.00.

Demitasse cup and saucer.

Lord Nelson Ware (Elijah Cotton Ltd.), c. 1930s.

Can with loop handle; chintz, Skylark.

$60.00 – 75.00.

Teacup and saucer.

Lord Nelson Ware, c. 1938.

Slightly waisted cup with angular handle; chintz, Rosetime.

$85.00 – 100.00.

Teacup and saucer.

John Maddock & Sons Ltd., c. 1891 – 1935.

Tapered cup with broken loop handle; colorful flowers in Imari colors.

$40.00 – 50.00.

Teacup and saucer.

Melba China Co., Ltd., c. 1948 – 1951.

Slightly flared cup with ring handle; floral pattern.

$35.00 – 45.00.

Demitasse cup and saucer.

Minton, c. 1945.

Slightly tapered, puffed cup with loop handle; floral garland design.

$40.00 – 50.00.

Same cup and saucer as bottom photo on page 225, only in red.

Teacup and saucer.

Moore Bros., c. 1891.

Quatrefoil, molded cup with feathered handle; floral transfer in each quadrant. (See mark #79.)

$50.00 – 60.00.

Teacup and saucer.

Myott, Son & Co., c. 1930+.

Sharply tapered earthenware cup with large angular handle; colorful bird transfer, artist signed, crazed. (See mark #81.)

$40.00 – 50.00.

Teacup and saucer.

New Chelsea China Company, c. 1951 – 1961.

Slightly flared and scalloped footed cup with "D" handle; lovely allover rose chintz-type pattern with black handle, rim, and foot.

$50.00 – 65.00.

Teacup and saucer.

New Chelsea China Company, c. 1951 – 1961.

Slightly ribbed and scalloped footed cup; blue floral decoration with gilt.

$35.00 – 45.00.

Teacup and saucer.

New Chelsea China Company, c. 1951 – 1961.

Slightly footed cup with coiled handle; orange enameled flowers with gilt.

$35.00 – 45.00.

Teacup and saucer.

Newport Pottery, c. 1932 – present.

London shape cup; Crocus pattern, "Bizarre" by Clarice Cliff.

$125.00 – 150.00.

Teacup and saucer.

Old Royal Bone China, c. 1930 – 1941.

Pedestal cup with "C" shaped handle; roses on light green ground.

$35.00 – 45.00.

Teacup and saucer.

Old Royal Bone China (Samson Smith), c. 1945 – 1963.

Footed cup with kidney-shaped handle; chintz polka-dot pattern. (See mark #84.)

$45.00 – 60.00.

Teacup and saucer.

Paragon, c. 1950s.

Puffed-out and ribbed at waist, footed with broken loop handle; Pembroke pattern.

$40.00 – 50.00.

Teacup, saucer, and dessert plate.

Paragon, 1957+.

Partially ribbed and footed cup; blue forget-me-nots outside and inside cup. (See mark #86.)

$75.00 – 95.00.

Teacup and saucer.

Paragon, c. 1952 – 1955.

Footed and scalloped cup with loop handle with inner spur and thumb rest; center rose design with band of cream and cobalt, gilt design.

$60.00 – 90.00.

Teacup and saucer.

Paragon, c. 1957+.

Footed, slightly scalloped cup; dramatic black and gold with red rose in center of cup and saucer.

$75.00 – 95.00.

Teacup and saucer.

Paragon, c. 1957+.

Footed with eight puffy flutes, ornate broken loop handle, crimped saucer; transfer of colorful mums.

$35.00 – 45.00.

Teacup and saucer.

Paragon, c. 1957+.

Footed and ribbed at bottom, crimped saucer; floral transfer.

$60.00 – 75.00.

Teacup and saucer.

Paragon, c. 1952 – 1955.

Scalloped cup and saucer, footed, loop handle with thumb rest and inner spur; lovely water lilies on pale green.

$40.00 – 50.00.

Demitasse cup and saucer.

Paragon, c. 1939 – 1949.

Scalloped can with thick gold handle; dark red and gold cobblestone motif, flowers inside saucer.

$35.00 – 45.00.

Teacup and saucer.

Paragon, c. 1939 – 1949.

Footed, scalloped cup with feather handle; green roses on pale green.

$35.00 – 45.00.

Teacup and saucer.

Paragon, c. 1952 – 1955.

Scalloped and footed cup with feathered handle; dramatic pink and black with rose inside cup and saucer.

$45.00 – 60.00.

Teacup and saucer.

Paragon, c. 1939 – 1949.

Scalloped and footed cup; flowers on aqua.

$35.00 – 45.00.

Teacup and saucer.

Paragon, c. 1939 – 1949.

Twenty-fluted cup with "C" handle, molded petals on saucer; floral transfer. (See mark #85.)

$40.00 – 50.00.

Teacup and saucer.

Paragon, c. 1939 – 1949.

Footed cup; loop handle with thumb rest and spur; rose in center of cup on pale yellow.

$35.00 – 45.00.

Teacup and saucer.

Paragon, c. 1957+.

Footed, fluted at bottom cup with broken loop handle; Nova Scotia Tartan.

$40.00 – 50.00.

Teacup and saucer.

Paragon, c. 1939 – 1949.

Footed and scalloped cup and saucer, high loop handle with thumb rest and inner spur; dramatic flowers on black ground, band of white on rim.

$45.00 – 60.00.

Teacup and saucer.

Paragon, c. 1957+.

Footed and scalloped cup; fruit inside and outside cup and saucer, gilt on rim.

$75.00 – 95.00.

Teacup and saucer.

Queen Anne (Shore & Coggins), c. 1950+.

Footed and fluted cup; Yule Tide.

$30.00 – 40.00.

Teacup and saucer.

Queen Anne, c. 1950+.

Scalloped and footed cup; gilt leaves on white, large red band in center of saucer and bottom of cup.

$30.00 – 40.00.

Teacup and saucer.

Queen Anne, c. 1950+.

Scalloped cup and saucer, handle-shape like the number 3; dark red and yellow roses.

$30.00 – 40.00.

Teacup and saucer.

Radford, Samuel, Ltd., c. 1938 – 1957.

Scalloped cup with "D" handle; lovely chintz pattern. (See mark #89.)

$75.00 – 95.00.

Teacup and saucer.

Regency China Ltd., c. 1953 – present.

Pear-shaped, slightly waisted cup with reinforced broken loop handle; peaches.

$30.00 – 35.00.

Teacup and saucer.

Regency China Ltd., c. 1950s.

Scalloped and waisted cup with reinforced loop handle with spurs and thumb rest; fruit transfer, gilding on foot rim, handle and rim of saucer. (See mark #90.)

$35.00 – 45.00.

Teacup and saucer.

Rosina China Co. Ltd., c. 1946 – 1948.

Slightly fluted, tapered cup with square handle; Heritage made for J. Crownford. (See mark #93.)

$40.00 – 50.00.

Teacup and saucer.

Rosina China Co. Ltd., c. 1952+.

Tapered and scalloped cup with gilt angular handle; large black band with lilies, row of gilt inside cup. (See mark #94.)

$40.00 – 50.00.

Teacup and saucer.

Rosina China Co. Ltd., c. 1960s – present.

Footed cup with ribbing near foot; "Birds of America," Series I.

$30.00 – 40.00.

Teacup and saucer.

Rosina China Co., c. 1952+.

Flared, footed cup with loop handle, bowl-shaped saucer; hand-painted flowers.

$35.00 – 45.00.

Teacup and saucer.

Rosina China Co., c. 1950s.

Flared, scalloped pedestal cup with French loop handle, scalloped saucer; outside of cup is gold, inside of cup and saucer have large mixed fruit design on light pink ground.

$50.00 – 75.00.

Snack set.

Royal Albert (Thomas C. Wild & Sons), c. 1945 – present.

Footed cup, puffed out at bottom, ornate broken loop handle with feathered thumb rest; Moss Rose.

$50.00 – 65.00.

Snack set.

Royal Albert, c. 1945 – present.

Footed, slightly fluted cup, kicked loop handle with thumb rest; Lucky Clover.

$40.00 – 60.00.

Teacup and saucer.

Royal Albert, c. 1945+.

Puffed eight-flute design, footed cup with "Question Mark" handle; Chrysanthemum, "Flower of the Month."

$30.00 – 40.00.

Teacup, saucer, and dessert plate.

Royal Albert, c. 1927 – 1934.

Pedestal cup with broken loop handle, thumb rest and inner spur; medallions of flowers on dark red.

$75.00 – 95.00.

Teacup and saucer.

Royal Albert, c. 1932.

Puffed-out and footed cup, slightly scalloped, reinforced loop handle with thumb rest; Royalty.

$60.00 – 90.00.

Teacup and saucer.

Royal Albert, c. 1945+.

Footed with eight puffy flutes, curled handle; deep turquoise with gilt trim.

$40.00 – 50.00.

Small teacup and saucer.

Royal Albert, c. 1945+.

Six-fluted and ribbed cup and saucer; forget-me-nots. (See mark #96.)

$40.00 – 50.00.

Teacup, saucer, and plate.

Royal Albert, current mark.

Footed, eight puffy flutes with broken loop handle; Brigadoon.

$50.00 – 75.00.

Teacup, saucer, and plate.

Royal Albert, current mark.

Footed, eight puffy flutes with broken loop handle; Lavender Rose. (See mark #97.)

$50.00 – 75.00.

Teacup and saucer.

Royal Albert, c. 1950s.

Footed, scalloped cup and saucer, reinforced loop handle; Night and Day pattern.

$40.00 – 50.00.

Teacup and saucer.

Royal Albert, c. 1950s.

Footed and fluted cup, ornate saucer; lovely dramatic floral transfer.

$35.00 – 40.00.

Teacup and saucer.

Royal Albert, Sonnet Series, c. 1960s.

Footed and puffed-out cup, unusual handle; Chaucer pattern.

$30.00 – 40.00.

Teacup and saucer.

Royal Albert, c. 1934.

Cup with unusual Art Deco handle; Dorothy pattern. (See mark #95.)

$60.00 – 90.00.

Teacup and saucer.

Royal Albert, Canada, Our Emblem's Dear Series, c. 1960s.

Footed and scalloped cup and saucer, ribbed at rim, fancy handle; each flower group represents a province.

$30.00 – 40.00.

Teacup and saucer.

Royal Albert, c. 1960s.

Scalloped, waisted, and footed cup with ribbing at bottom, broken loop handle with thumb rest; "Cameo Series – Memento."

$40.00 – 50.00.

Teacup and saucer.

Royal Albert, c. 1960s – present.

Footed and scalloped cup with loop handle with thumb rest; American Beauty.

$35.00 – 45.00.

Teacup and saucer.

Royal Albert, c. 1945.

Eight-lobed, footed cup, loop handle with thumb rest; Blossom Time.

$40.00 – 50.00.

Teacup, saucer, and dessert plate.

Royal Albert, c. 1945+.

Puffy, fluted, footed cup with reinforced loop handle with thumb rest; Violets, #2 in "Flower of the Month" series.

$60.00 – 75.00.

Coffee cup and saucer.

Royal Chelsea (New Chelsea Porcelain Co.), c. 1950s.

Ribbed cup with angular handle; autumn leaves with forget-me-nots.

$30.00 – 35.00.

Teacup and saucer.

Royal Dover, Current.

Ribbed cup and saucer, angular handle; wild roses, gold rim. (See mark #100.)

$35.00 – 40.00.

Teacup and saucer.

Royal Grafton, c. 1950+.

Slightly waisted cup with loop handle; solid turquoise, gilt rims on saucer and cup.

$30.00 – 35.00.

Teacup and saucer.

Royal Kent (James Kent, Ltd.), current.

Slightly scalloped cup with ear-shaped handle; ivy design. (See mark #101.)

$30.00 – 35.00.

Teacup and saucer.

Royal Stafford China, England, c. 1952.

Sixteen flutes, French loop handle; Carnation.

$35.00 – 45.00.

Teacup and saucer.

Royal Stafford China, Tartan Series, c. 1952 – present.

Footed cup with kicked loop handle; Maclean pattern. (See mark #102.)

$40.00 – 50.00.

Teacup and saucer.

Royal Stafford China, c. 1960s – present.

Scalloped, gilt, footed cup with kicked loop handle; cream and dark red bands with gilt scrolling.

$35.00 – 45.00.

Teacup and saucer.

Royal Standard (Chapmans Longton Ltd.), c. 1949 – present.

Ribbed cup with zigzag handle; bright red floral transfer. (See mark #103.)

$35.00 – 45.00.

Teacup and saucer.

Royal Standard, c. 1949+.

Slightly fluted and tapered cup with foot trimmed in gold, gilt trim on saucer; aqua rose and polka dots.

$40.00 – 50.00.

Teacup and saucer.

Royal Standard, c. 1930 – 1964.

Slightly flared cup with "D" shaped handle; chintz Virginia Stock pattern.

$50.00 – 75.00.

Teacup and saucer.

Royal Stuart (Stevenson, Spencer & Co. Ltd.), c. 1950+.

Twelve-fluted cup and saucer, unusual flower handle; floral transfer.

$75.00 – 95.00.

Teacup and saucer.

Royal Vale, c. 1962+.

Footed and slightly waisted cup with broken loop handle, scalloped saucer; blue bachelor buttons.

$30.00 – 40.00.

Teacup and saucer.

Royal Vale, c. 1962+.

Scalloped cup with broken loop handle with thumb rest; fall leaves transfer.

$30.00 – 40.00.

Teacup and saucer.

Royal Winton, (Grimwades, Ltd.), c. 1934 – 1950.

Footed cup with loop handle; hand-painted cows, mountain and water scene with tartan ribbon decorating cup and saucer.

$60.00 – 75.00.

Teacup and saucer.

Royal Winton, c. 1934 – 1950.

Slightly flared cup, floral-shaped handle; iridescent yellow flowing into deep burgundy.

$75.00 – 95.00.

Teacup and saucer.

Royal Winton, c. 1950s.

Raleigh shape; chintz, Nantwich.

$100.00 – 125.00.

Teacup and saucer.

Royal Winton, c. 1936.

Ascot shape; chintz, Queen Anne.

$60.00 – 75.00.

Teacup and saucer.

Royal Winton, c. 1930 – 1960.

Eton shape; chintz, Old Cottage.

$75.00 – 95.00.

Teacup and saucer.

Royal Winton, c. 1936.

Ascot shape; chintz, Victorian.

$60.00 – 75.00.

Teacup and saucer.

Royal Winton, c. 1932.

Chintz, Summertime.

$75.00 – 100.00.

Teacup (part of stacking teapot).

Royal Winton, c. 1951.

Chintz, Balmoral pattern. Cup alone.

$50.00 – 65.00.

Stacking teapot.

Royal Winton, c. 1951.

Balmoral.

$900.00 – 1,000.00.

Teacup and saucer.

Royal Winton, c. 1950s.

Raleigh shape; English Manor House pattern.

$75.00 – 100.00.

Teacup and saucer.

Salisbury Crown China Co., c. 1951.

Fluted cup, scalloped saucer, angular handle with flat thumb rest; rose transfer.

$30.00 – 40.00.

Teacup and saucer.

Salisbury Crown China, c. 1930s.

Slightly scalloped cup with loop handle; lovely pink floral transfer.

$30.00 – 50.00.

Teacup, saucer, and dessert plate.

Shelley, c. 1925 – 1940.

Lily of the Valley.

$100.00 – 125.00.

Teacups and saucers.

Shelley, c. 1925 – 1940.

Six flutes; pale blue with pink handle and pale pink with blue handle.

$45.00 – 60.00 each.

Teacup and saucer.

Shelley, c. 1925 – 1940.

Six-fluted cup and saucer; Regency.

$50.00 – 60.00.

Teacup and saucer.

Shelley, c. 1945 – 1960.

Six-fluted cup; large gold star design on black.

$75.00 – 100.00.

Demitasse cup and saucer.

Shelley, c. 1945 – 1966.

Fourteen-fluted cup and saucer; Rose and Red Daisy.

$50.00 – 65.00.

Teacup and saucer.

Shelley, c. 1945 – 1966.

Henley shape; variation of Rosebud pattern.

$45.00 – 60.00.

Demitasse cup and saucer.

Shelley, c. 1945 – 1966.

Delicately fluted and ribbed cup with loop handle; Primrose pattern.

$50.00 – 65.00.

Teacup and saucer.

Shelley, c. 1945 – 1966.

Dainty shape; violets.

$60.00 – 80.00.

Demitasse cup and saucer.

Shelley, c. 1945 – 1966.

Puffy-shaped cup with six flutes; unusual scenic transfer decoration.

$50.00 – 65.00.

Teacup and saucer.

Shelley, c. 1945 – 1966.

Corset-shaped, scalloped, loop handle with thumb rest; Woodland.

$50.00 – 75.00.

View of saucer above.

Demitasse cup and saucer.

Shelley, c. 1945 – 1966.

Dainty shape with loop handle; Pansy.

$50.00 – 75.00.

Teacup and saucer.

Shelley, c. 1945 – 1966.

Corset-shaped, loop handle with thumb rest; Daffodil Time.

$50.00 – 75.00.

Teacup and saucer.

Shelley, c. 1945 – 1966.

Fourteen-flute shape with loop handle; cherries.

$50.00 – 75.00.

Demitasse cup and saucer.

Shelley, c. 1945 – 1966.

Henley shape; Summer Glory.

$100.00 – 125.00.

Teacup and saucer.

Shelley, c. 1945 – 1966.

Oleander shape with gilt loop handle and foot; variation of Blue Rock pattern.

$75.00 – 95.00.

Demitasse cup and saucer.

Shelley, c. 1945 – 1966.

Mocha shape with dainty detail; Regency.

$45.00 – 65.00.

Teacup and saucer.

Shelley, c. 1945 – 1966.

Henley shape; white polka dots on dark red, gilded foot and rims of cup and saucer.

$75.00 – 100.00.

Teacup and saucer.

Shelley, c. 1945 – 1966.

Oleander shape with gilt handle and foot; Melody pattern on inside of cup.

$100.00 – 125.00.

Teacup and saucer.

Shelley, c. 1945 – 1966.

Chester shape; chintz Country Side pattern.

$100.00 – 125.00.

Teacup and saucer.

Shelley, c. 1945 – 1966.

Queen Anne shape; chintz Summer Glory.

$125.00 – 145.00.

Teacup and saucer.

Shelley, c. 1945 – 1966.

Chester shape; chintz Melody pattern.

$125.00 – 135.00.

Teacup and saucer.

Shelley, c. 1945 – 1966.

Oleander shape; chintz Country Side pattern on inside of cup.

$125.00 – 150.00.

Teacup and saucer.

Shelley, c. 1945 – 1966.

Oleander shape; chintz Primrose.

$125.00 – 150.00.

Teacup and saucer.

Shelley, c. 1945 – 1966.

Chester shape; chintz Rock Garden.

$125.00 – 135.00.

Teacup and saucer.

Shelley, c. 1925 – 1945.

Queen Anne shape; Cottage.

$75.00 – 95.00.

Teacup and saucer.

Shelley, c. 1945 – 1966.

Dainty shape; Dainty Blue.

$75.00 – 100.00.

Demitasse cup and saucer.

Shelley, c. 1945 – 1966.

Dainty shape; Dainty Blue.

$60.00 – 90.00.

Teacup and saucer.

Shelley, c. 1945 – 1966.

Dainty shape; Dainty Pink.

$75.00 – 100.00.

Demitasse cup and saucer.

Shelley, c. 1945 – 1966.

Dainty shape; Dainty Pink.

$60.00 – 90.00.

Teacup and saucer.

Shelley, c. 1945 – 1966.

Dainty shape; Dainty Mauve.

$90.00 – 125.00.

Teacup and saucer.

Shelley, c. 1945 – 1966.

Dainty shape; Dainty Yellow.

$75.00 – 100.00.

Demitasse cup and saucer.

Shelley, c. 1945 – 1966.

Dainty shape; Dainty Green.

$60.00 – 90.00.

Teacup and saucer.

Shelley, c. 1945 – 1966.

Dainty shape; Dainty Brown.

$75.00 – 100.00.

Teacup and saucer.

Shelley, c. 1945 – 1966.

Dainty shape; Heavenly Blue.

$60.00 – 80.00.

Teacup and saucer.

Shelley, c. 1925 – 1940.

Footed cup with French loop handle; pale pink ground with fruit inside cup. (See mark #110.)

$50.00 – 75.00.

Teacup, saucer, and dessert plate.

Shelley, c. 1925 – 1940.

Twelve-fluted cup and saucer; Dainty Blue.

$125.00 – 150.00.

Teacup, saucer, and dessert plate.

Shelley, c. 1925 – 1940.

Twelve-fluted cup and saucer; Morning Glory.

$125.00 – 150.00.

Teacup and saucer.

Stanley Fine Bone China (Charles Aminson), c. 1953 – 1962.

Footed cup with coiled loop handle; lovely rose transfer.

$30.00 – 40.00.

Teacup and saucer.

Stanley China, c. 1953 – 1962.

Slightly scalloped and waisted cup, curled, broken loop handle; colorful rose decal inside and out.

$30.00 – 40.00.

Teacup and saucer.

Taylor & Kent Ltd., c. 1939 – 1949.

Footed, scalloped cup with unusual handle; bright blue floral transfer. (See mark #114.)

$35.00 – 45.00.

Teacup and saucer.

Watcombe Pottery Company, c. 1875 – 1901.

Straight – sided cup with fat loop handle; Torquay motto ware, "A Cup of Tea is very refreshing."

$50.00 – 75.00.

Front view of above teacup.

Teacup and saucer.

Wedgwood, c. 1920+.

Footed cup with French loop handle; Gold Florentine.

$40.00 – 55.00.

Teacup, saucer, and dessert plate.

Wedgwood, c. 1960.

Slightly flared, footed cup with French loop handle; blue with gold leafy trim.

$75.00 – 95.00.

Demitasse cup and saucer.

Wedgwood, c. 1950s.

Blue jasper ware can with loop handle; classical scenes.

$40.00 – 60.00.

Demitasse cup and saucer.

Wedgwood, c. 1910 – 1920.

Can with loop handle, deep saucer; black with silver deposit.

$45.00 – 60.00.

Teacup and saucer.

Wedgwood, c. 1960s.

Footed creamware cup, ribbed on bottom half, backwards "C" handle; Conway.

$30.00 – 40.00.

Teacup and saucer.

Wedgwood, c. 1901 – 1919.

Footed cup with kicked loop handle; Florentine pattern.

$50.00 – 75.00.

Demitasse cup and saucer.

Wedgwood, c. 1950s.

Footed creamware cup with feathered loop handle; six – panel saucer; Husk pattern made for Williamsburg.

$25.00 – 35.00.

Demitasse cup and saucer.

Wedgwood, c. 1892.

Slightly waisted cup molded at bottom, square handle; gold floral decoration on white.

$45.00 – 60.00.

Demitasse cup and saucer.

Wedgwood, c. 1878 – 1900.

Tapered cup with angular kicked handle; lovely gilt decoration with floral transfer.

$45.00 – 60.00.

Demitasse cup and saucer.

Wedgwood, c. 1950s.

Waisted and footed cup with loop handle; Celadon pattern.

$30.00 – 40.00.

Demitasse cup and saucer.

Wedgwood, c. 1920 – 1930.

Slightly waisted cup with loop handle; blue flowers and green leaves.

$45.00 – 55.00.

Demitasse cup and saucer.

Wedgwood, c. 1934 – present.

Can with square handle; Blue Willow pattern on creamware body.

$30.00 – 40.00.

Teacup and saucer.

Wedgwood, c. 1934 – present.

Slightly scalloped, round cup with loop handle; blue and white decoration, Yale commemorative.

$50.00 – 60.00.

Demitasse cup and saucer.

Wedgwood, c. 1920 – 1930.

Can with loop handle; Eluria pattern, silver luster in creamware.

$35.00 – 45.00.

Demitasse cup and saucer.

Wedgwood, c. 1920 – 1930.

Can with loop handle; gold leaf decoration on white ground.

$35.00 – 45.00.

Teacup and saucer.

Windsor, c. 1950s.

Footed cup with broken loop handle with thumb rest; blue flowers with raised orange seeds in middle.

$30.00 – 40.00.

Demitasse cup and saucer.

Royal Worcester, c. 1944 – 1955.

Bernina pattern.

$35.00 – 50.00.

Teacup and saucer.

Royal Worcester, c. 1930.

Slightly scalloped cup and saucer, feathered, broken loop handle; cobalt blue band on rim with ribbon of gilt leaves.

$45.00 – 60.00.

Teacup and saucer.

Royal Worcester, c. 1924.

Slightly footed and flared cup with angular handle; garland of roses and pineapples inside cup and on saucer; yellow band on rim.

$50.00 – 65.00.

Demitasse cup and saucer.

Royal Worcester, c. 1950s.

Ribbed and scalloped can and saucer with loop handle; Lavina pattern. (See mark #122.)

$35.00 – 45.00.

Demitasse cup and saucer.

Royal Worcester, c. 1930.

Slightly flared, footed cup with angular handle; brilliant floral transfer in center of saucer; hand-gilded tracery all over, handkerchief motif.

$100.00 – 125.00.

Demitasse cup and saucer.

Royal Worcester, c. 1960s.

Can with bamboo handle, floral transfer.

$40.00 – 50.00.

Demitasse cup and saucer.

Royal Worcester, c. 1944 – 1955.

Sixteen-ribbed cup and saucer with loop handle; Dunrobin pattern. (See mark #121.)

$40.00 – 50.00.

"Teacup Fairy," Royal Worcester cup and saucer, from authors' personal collection.
$300.00 – 350.00.

MINIATURES

Miniatures have been made for thousands of years. Tiny toys, vases, jars, and other items have been uncovered by archeologists and explorers, and these small treasures are housed in museums throughout the world.

Little things have a fascination for everyone, and the collecting of miniatures has been a popular pastime since the eighteenth century. It is still one of the world's leading hobbies, and many cup and saucer collectors are miniature enthusiasts.

DOLLHOUSE SIZE

Dollhouse-size miniatures are the smallest — usually scaled an inch to a foot. During the late seventeenth century, miniature china dinnerware sets were produced in England and Europe to furnish miniature rooms for adults. By the nineteenth century many more companies produced these sets, and they were made for children's and adults' dollhouses.

Mary of Teck, wife of George V of Great Britain, King from 1910 to 1936, was an avid collector of dollhouses and miniatures. Because of her interest, the hobby regained popularity in the 1930s through the 1950s, and early dollhouse-size miniatures are now quite rare, usually housed in museums or private collections.

Beginning in 1950, miniature tea sets were mass-produced in Japan and China; they are still being exported today. Many of these new sets are of average to poor quality and feature floral decoration as well as the popular Blue Willow and Blue Onion patterns.

CHILD'S SIZE

"So now for a feast,
Bread and Jam at the least,
And there's cake on a dish
For those who may wish;
Milk and water and sugar and very weak tea."

(Eliza Kearny, *At Home Again*, 1883, *Victoria Entertaining*)

During the Victorian era, wealthy families furnished nurseries for their children. While they partook of tea in the parlor, the children were served in the nursery. This practice required child-size tea sets. Teacups were made to hold three or four ounces, just the right size for three-year-olds and up.

Three and four ounce miniatures were produced in England, Germany, and the United States in the nineteenth century. Manufacturers decorated these pieces with animal themes, nursery rhyme and fairy tale characters, children's activities, and the artware of famous illustrators, such as Kate Greenaway.

ABC ware, dinnerware made for children on which the alphabet appears, is eagerly collected today. First made in the early nineteenth century, Staffordshire ABC ware included over more than 700 patterns. In the case of a small item, such as a cup, the alphabet contained too many characters to fit, so the English manufacturers solved this problem by making the letters smaller or by only using a few letters.

Child's size miniatures are the most abundant and reasonably priced today. American production of children's ware reached a peak during World War II before the less costly Japanese ware became available.

SALESMAN'S SAMPLES

Salesman's samples are actual models made by ceramics companies. They often displayed advertising messages intended to boost the sales of their products. They were accompanied by a carrying case, the indisputable mark of a salesman's sample. These samples were shown to wholesalers and retailers so that they could place an order for a line of tea ware. These samples are rare and highly priced.

TOY-SIZE

A size of miniatures larger than the dollhouse-size but smaller than child's size has con

fused collectors and dealers alike. Miniatures in this size are often mistakenly referred to as salesmen's samples.

These toy-size miniatures served several purposes. First, they were made to collect and display in a cabinet. Second, they were made to teach manners and social graces to children of wealthy families in the eighteenth and nineteenth centuries. These teacups and saucers were frequently decorated with historical scenes and mottoes. Finally, as the name implies, they could be used as toys for children to enjoy.

These toy-size cups and saucers were made in the same forms, shapes, and styles as the full-size ones of the period. They were manufactured as early as the sixteenth century in China and western Europe. The potters of Nuremberg, Germany, were famous for their miniature bowls, vases, and dinner services decorated in vivid colors. Early tea bowls and saucers made by Meissen occasionally turn up. Small pottery items decorated in blue and white were produced in the Netherlands in the seventeenth century and were introduced to England in the 1690s. Soon "baby house wares" were part of the normal stock of the Staffordshire potteries.

Miniature creamware, stoneware, and porcelain cups and saucers were widely produced in the nineteenth century, and signed examples by Coalport, Minton, Spode, and Worcester are highly sought. Coffee cans made by Vienna and Sevres can be found with exquisite hand-painted scenic and floral reserves. Miniature cups and saucers, often in the popular quatrefoil shape, were decorated by the Dresden studios in the late nineteenth century.

The most common examples of toy-size cups and saucers found in the marketplace today date from the twentieth century. In France several companies in the Limoges area produced them around the turn of the century and still make them today. Examples of lovely molded cups with leafy feet and unusual shaped handles were manufactured by the R.S. Prussia Company, c. 1900. In England miniature tea sets with trays, which were exact replicas of full-size sets, were made by Shelley, Crown Staffordshire, Copeland Spode, Wedgwood, Royal Crown Derby, and Coalport. The Royal Crown Derby examples decorated in the Imari patterns are highly desirable. Probably the hottest miniature cups and saucers in the marketplace today are those made by Shelley, and the price for a cup and saucer can reach as high as $250.00 – 300.00. In the United States Leneige Company and Gort China made miniature cups and saucers in the 1930s – 1950s.

"With all my Love." Postcard, c.1906.

Teacup and saucer.

Dresden, Helena Wolfsohn, c. 1843 – 1883.

Rounded cup with Old English handle; hand-painted scenes alternating with floral panels. (See mark #35.)

$150.00 – 200.00.

Teacup and saucer.

Dresden, Richard Klemm, c. 1888 – 1916.

Cup in Royal Flute shape with twisted feather handle, deep saucer; alternating hand-painted scenes and floral medallions. (See mark #31.)

$200.00 – 225.00.

Coffee can and saucer.

Dresden, Helena Wolfsohn, c. 1886.

Can with loop handle, deep saucer; beautiful hand-painted birds, bugs, and butterflies with gilt.

$275.00 – 325.00.

Teacup and saucer.

Dresden, Thieme, Carl, c. 1890s.

Round cup with loop handle; alternating hand-painted scenes and flowers.

$150.00 – 175.00.

Teacup and saucer.

Dresden, Lamm, A., c. 1887.

Quatrefoil cup with wishbone handle; alternating hand-painted scenes and flowers, gilt decoration around rim.

$200.00 – 225.00.

Teacup and saucer.

Eberthal Qualitats Porzellan Co., West Germany, c. 1949 – 1970s.

Footed cup with fancy coiled handle; bird and flowers.

$40.00 – 50.00.

Coffee can and saucer.

Meissen, c. 1800 – 1850.

Can with loop handle, saucer bowl; polychrome Oriental design.

$400.00 – 500.00.

Teacup and saucer.

Meissen, c. 1800 – 1850.

Cup with loop handle; applied flowers outside cup and bottom saucer.

$500.00 – 550.00+.

Demitasse cup and saucer.

Royal Bayreuth, c. 1887 – 1902.

Figural cup in shape of clover flower, saucer in leaf form, angular handle.

$400.00 – 450.00.

Teacup and saucer.

Victoria Porcelain Factory, c. 1891 – 1918.

Scalloped cup and saucer; gilt, scrolled decoration on dark pink shading.

$50.00 – 75.00.

Coffee cup and saucer.

Victorian Porcelain Factory, c. 1891 – 1918.

Child's scalloped and waisted cup with kicked loop handle, six-sided star-shaped saucer; gold decoration on dark green.

$50.00 – 75.00.

Coffee cup and saucer.

Bing & Grondahl, c. 1948.

Straight-sided child's cup with loop handle; gray with gilt trim.

$40.00 – 50.00.

Teacup and saucer.

Arabia Porcelain Factory, Finland, c. 1900 – 1910.

Slightly flared cup with loop handle with thumb rest; blue and white transfer of woman sailing between two buildings.

$50.00 – 75.00.

Teacup and saucer attached.

Limoges, Bawo and Dotter, c. 1896 – 1900.

Quatrefoil cup with loop handle; hand-painted blue forget-me-nots; 1" x 1½".

$50.00 – 75.00.

Teacup and saucer attached.

Limoges, Bawo and Dotter, c. 1896 – 1900.

Quatrefoil cup with loop handle; hand-painted roses; 1" x 1½".

$50.00 – 75.00.

Coffee cup and saucer.

Limoges, Giraud, A., c. 1920s.

Can with loop handle; band of flowers on gold. (See mark #62.)

$100.00 – 125.00.

Coffee cup and saucer.

Unmarked, probably French, c. 1920s.

Swirled cup with gilt loop handle, scalloped saucer; hand-painted roses, gilt decoration inside rim.

$125.00 – 150.00.

Child's teacup and saucer.

Nippon, c. 1891 – 1921.

Cup with loop handle; yellow with black and white trim.

$30.00 – 40.00.

Teacup and saucer.

Reproduction of Crown Derby mark, probably Occupied Japan, c. 1949.

Quatrefoil shape with wishbone handle; Imari pattern with gold interior.

$50.00 – 75.00.

Teacup and saucer.

Royal Adderley, c. 1960s.

Round cup with loop handle; flower bud transfer.

$50.00 – 75.00.

Teacup and saucer.

Royal Adderley, c. 1955 – present.

Round cup with loop handle; floral transfer.

$50.00 – 75.00.

Teacup and saucer.

Coalport, c. 1920 – 1939.

Indian Tree pattern.

$125.00 – 150.00.

Teacups and saucers.

Coalport, 1960 – present.

Round cups with loop handles, Ming Rose pattern, one with gilt trim. (See mark #18.)

$75.00 – 95.00 each.

Teacup and saucer.

Coalport, 1960 – present.

Round cup with loop handle, Indian Tree pattern.

$75.00 – 95.00.

Teacup and saucer.

Coalport, c. 1960s.

Rounded cup with loop handle; Blue Willow.

$75.00 – 95.00.

Teacup and saucer.

W. T. Copeland, Spode Works, c. 1940 – 1956.

Rounded cup with loop handle; floral transfer.

$75.00 – 100.00.

Same as above in different colors.

Teacup and saucer.

W. T. Copeland, Spode Works, c. 1940 – 1956.

Round cup with loop handle, green leafy transfer.

$75.00 – 100.00.

Teacup and saucer.

W. T. Copeland, c. 1940 – 1956.

Round cup with loop handle; paisley star design.

$75.00 – 100.00.

Teacup and saucer.

Royal Crown Derby, c. 1923.

London-shaped cup; floral decoration.

$150.00 – 175.00.

Teacup and saucer.

Royal Crown Derby, c. 1920s.

Cup with London-type handle; hand-painted flowers in Imari colors.

$125.00 – 150.00.

Teacup and saucer.

Crown Staffordshire, c. 1920s.

Hand-painted flowers, cobalt and gilt.

$150.00 – 175.00.

Teacup and saucer.

Crown Staffordshire, c. 1906 – 1929.

Slightly flared cup with brown French loop handle; enameled Chinese design with pagodas.

$100.00 – 125.00.

Teacup and saucer.

Crown Staffordshire, c. 1906 – 1929.

Slightly flared cup with turquoise French loop handle; rose transfer on white.

$100.00 – 125.00.

Teacup and saucer.

Crown Staffordshire, c. 1920s.

Slightly flared cup with kicked loop handle; florals.

$100.00 – 125.00.

Teacup and saucer.

Denton China (Longton Ltd.), c. 1945 – present.

Flared cup with fat loop handle; hand-painted scene.

$100.00 – 125.00.

Coffee cup and saucer.

The Foley China Co., c. 1890 – 1910.

Straight-sided cup with loop handle; "Welsh Tea party" on cup and "Welsh Spinner" on saucer.

$175.00 – 200.00.

Teacup and saucer.

Foley Bone China (E. Brain & Co. Ltd.), c. 1945 – 1963.

Round cup with loop handle; hand-painted floral.

$100.00 – 150.00.

Teacup and saucer.

Foley Bone China, c. 1945 – 1963.

Slightly flared cup with loop handle; hand-painted floral.

$100.00 – 150.00.

Teacup and saucer.

Foley, c. 1921 – 1929.

Cup with loop handle; floral transfer.

$100.00 – 125.00.

Coffee can and saucer.

Grainger, Worcester, c. 1901.

Can with kicked square handle; hand-painted birds on ivory finish.

$250.00 – 275.00.

Teacup and saucer.

Grosvenor China Ltd., c. 1961 – 1969.

Cup with broken loop handle; paisley chintz pattern.

$100.00 – 150.00.

Teacup and saucer.

Grosvenor China Ltd., c. 1961 – 1969.

Flared cup with broken loop handle; chintz pattern.

$100.00 – 150.00.

Teacup and saucer.

Healacraft Bone China, made in England, c. 1980.

Scalloped, footed cup; applied yellow rose. (See mark #44.)

$40.00 – 50.00.

Teacup and saucer.

Hammersley & Co., c. 1932 – present.

Flared cup with coiled loop handle; floral transfer.

$50.00 – 75.00.

Teacup and saucer.

Hammersley & Co., c. 1932 – present.

Flared cup with gold loop handle; violets.

$50.00 – 75.00.

Teacup and saucer.

Liverpool Road Pottery, c. 1930s.

Fluted cup with pinched loop handle; hand-painted fern design.

$75.00 – 100.00.

Teacup and saucer.

Minton, c. 1912 – 1950.

Gold rimmed with flared lip, loop handle; floral transfer.

$100.00 – 125.00.

Teacup and saucer.

Oakley China, made in England, unidentified mark.

Slightly scalloped cup with loop handle; floral transfer.

$50.00 – 75.00.

Teacup and saucer.

Rosina China Co., Ltd., c. 1948 – 1952.

Tapered double waisted cup with squashed handle; paisley chintz pattern.

$75.00 – 100.00.

Teacup and saucer.

Royal Albert, c. 1970.

Footed cup with angular handle; Lily of the Valley, May Anniversary.

$40.00 – 60.00.

Teacup and saucer.

Royal Sutherland (Hudson & Middleton Ltd.), c. 1947 – 1959.

Ribbed cup with broken loop handle; floral transfer. (See mark #104.)

$50.00 – 75.00.

Teacup and saucer.

Royal Sutherland (Hudson & Middleton Ltd.), c. 1947 – 1959.

Ribbed cup with broken loop handle; holly design.

$40.00 – 60.00.

Teacup and saucer.

Sanford, c. 1960s.

Fluted cup and saucer, gold pinched loop handle; floral decoration.

$40.00 – 60.00.

Coffee cup and saucer.

Shelley, c. 1945 – 1966.

Straight-sided cup with loop handle; Rosebud.

$175.00 – 200.00+.

Teacup and saucer.

Shelley, c. 1945 – 1966.

Dainty shape with loop handle; Dainty Mauve.

$200.00 – 250.00.

Coffee cup and saucer.

Shelley, c. 1945 – 1966.

Straight-sided cup with loop handle; Blue Rock.

$175.00 – 200.00+.

Coffee cup and saucer.

Shelley, c. 1945 – 1966.

Straight-sided cup with loop handle; souvenir of Southampton and Bermuda.

$150.00 – 175.00.

Coffee cup and saucer.

Shelley, c. 1945 – 1966.

Straight-sided cup with loop handle; Charm.

$175.00 – 200.00.

Teacup and saucer.

Shelley, c. 1945 – 1966.

Straight-sided cup with loop handle; Lily of the Valley.

$175.00 – 200.00+.

Coffee cup and saucer.

Shelley, c. 1945 – 1966.

Straight-sided cup with loop handle; Rock Garden.

$300.00 – 350.00+.

Teacup and saucer.

Shelley, c. 1945 – 1966.

Straight-sided cup with loop handle; Primrose.

$175.00 – 200.00+.

Teacup and saucer.

Shelley, c. 1945 – 1966.

Straight-sided cup with loop handle; Rose-Pansy Forget-Me-Not pattern.

$175.00 – 200.00+.

Teacup and saucer.

Shelley, c. 1945 – 1966.

Straight-sided cup with loop handle; Harebell.

$175.00 – 200.00+.

Teacup and saucer.

Unidentified mark.

Child's ribbed cup and saucer, rustic handle; floral transfer.

$40.00 – 50.00.

Coffee cup and saucer.

Unmarked.

Tapered scalloped cup with loop handle; outline of violet flower on white, gilded rim.

$50.00 – 75.00.

MUSTACHE CUPS AND SAUCERS

THE MUSTACHE RAGE

There's an old Spanish saying that "a kiss without a mustache is like an egg without salt." For many centuries, European monarchs had beards or mustaches. In France, members of the royal court had their own personal mustache barbers who spent hours pruning, waxing, dyeing, and perfuming their facial hair. In 1883 Mrs. Guy de Maupassant wrote the following words to her girlfriend:

"Truly a man without a mustache is not a man.

Never allow yourself to be embraced by a man without a mustache; his lips have no taste, none whatever!! There is no longer that charm, that softness, and that — pepper, yes, that pepper of the true kiss. The mustache is the spice of it...

In a mustache, a man preserves at the same time his attraction and his finesse. And of what varied appearance they are, these mustaches!

Some are curved, curled, and coquettish. These seem to love women above all things!!

Some are pointed, sharp as a needle, wicked. These have a preference for wine, horses, and fights...It is romantic, gallant, and brave. It dips itself daintily in wine and knows how to laugh with elegance.

Long live the mustache!"

During the battle of Waterloo in England in 1815, most young cavalry officers wore mustaches. The phrase "old mustache" originated in referring to a soldier during this time. The English wore long and drooping mustaches called "Piccadilly weepers."

Mustaches were popular with soldiers in the United States also, especially during the war with Mexico in 1846 – 1848. During the Gold Rush men found it difficult to shave because of the rugged life style. The "handlebar" was the rage in the Gay Nineties and was satirized in the song by Stephen Foster and George Cooper, *If You've Only Got a Mustache.*

Mustaches were curled, waxed, and touched-up with dye. Some men used rollers and nets to hold the curl at night. It is easy to understand why after such painstaking care the wearers of these mustaches were not eager to dampen their pride and joy while drinking liquids from a cup. This gave rise to an important new dinnerware item — the mustache cup.

GROWTH OF MUSTACHE CUPS

The mustache cup was the most prized possession of the mustache wearer. It was a drinking cup featuring a raised lip guard attached to the rim of the cup which prevented the mustache from touching the liquid.

The first mustache cup was designed in 1830 by Harvey Adams at a pottery in Longton, Stoke-on-Trent, England. Hammersley became Adams' partner in 1860, and in 1875, Adams retired. The Hammersley family has continued operating the company up to the present time.

Mustache cups were originally called "Napoleons," named after the French soldiers who wore small beards and mustaches, "Napoleons," after the Franco-Prussian War. Among the aristocracy, each gentleman had his own china maker, whose identity was carefully shielded. The guard across the top was designed from a mold in the exact shape and size of the nobleman's mustache. There was one clever young French count who ordered his silversmith to make a personal mustache guard for him. It fit into an elaborate case similar to a snuff box, in which he could carry the guard with him in his pocket. It had springs at both ends so it could be pushed together and inserted into any cup. Once the spring was released, it locked tightly at both sides. This gentleman didn't want to take the chance of dining at a party where the necessary cups weren't provided.

During the early years of production, mustache cups and saucers were sold as individual

items, but as the nineteenth century progressed they were sold with complete sets of tableware. It is said that Mrs. John Aster had a beautiful set of 12 mustache cups and saucers that matched her dinner set. Mustache cups that belonged to porcelain dinner sets, such as Haviland, were usually small and dainty, while those for everyday use were large and heavy. Mustache cups were used to drink coffee, tea, and even hot chocolate.

Mustache cups became popular in the United States during the mid-nineteenth century. German potters produced vast quantities of mustache cups for export to the United States. By the 1880s and well into the 1890s elaborately decorated sets were produced by ceramic factories in many countries. It was considered good taste to give these cups as gifts to both husbands and wives. Of course the cups for the wife did not have the guard, but they matched the husband's cup in every other way. These matching sets were usually displayed rather than used.

Mustache cups reached their peak of popularity during the 1890s but were made well into the first quarter of the twentiethth century. The last time mustache cups were advertised in this country for practical use was in a Sears Roebuck catalog in 1904.

VARIETY OF FORMS AND DECORATION

Potters used their imagination in creating many unique and fascinating forms and decorations. Mustache cups were made from earthenware, porcelain, stoneware, tin, and silverplate in many shapes and sizes, ranging from tiny demitasse cups to large farmer's cups holding up to a quart of liquid. One jumbo mustache cup with a smiling fat man is inscribed, "I am not greedy, but I like a lot."

Early cups were bowl-shaped, cylindrical, six-or eight-sided, ribbed, melon-shaped, and kettle-shaped. Handles were made in many different forms. Highly collectible are mustache cups with handles formed as snakes, insects, birds, twisted ropes, fans, and cherubs.

The saucers matched or harmonized with the cups both in shape and decoration. Early saucers were deep, while later examples became more shallow, like regular saucers.

Many mustache cups, especially those made in Germany, have luster grounds, which were Victorian favorites. Pink luster was the most popular. Other ground colors frequently used were pale green, yellow, sky blue, lavender, coral, cobalt, and gold. Many German mustache cups are richly encrusted with ornate forms of applied decoration.

Mustache cups can be found decorated with landscapes, hunting scenes, animals and birds, flowers, and interesting geometric designs. Portrait mustache cups are very rare and highly desirable.

Mustache cups with mottoes or expressions were a fad in the late nineteenth century. The expressions were written in enamel or gold, or molded in relief. Some examples are Remember Me, Love the Giver, Forget-Me-Not, A Present, Birthday Greetings. Others had Father, Papa, and Mother. Numerous souvenir mustache cups were made, often on a pink ground. Mustache cups were made to commemorate historical events and royal coronations.

RARITIES

In her helpful book, *Mustache Cups*, Dorothy Hammond says, "Many collectors consider French mustache cups to be the aristocrats in the field. Then there are those who prefer German-made cups made by Meissen or R.S. Prussia. Rarities that advanced collectors seek out are majolica, Imari, Rose Medallion, Sunderland Luster, Belleek, Crown Derby, and Wedgwood."

Staffordshire mustache cups decorated with transfer printed designs are scarce and command high prices. Matched cups and saucers made by Limoges, Rosenthal, Royal Worcester, and Royal Bayreuth are also becoming hard to find. Silverplated mustache cups and saucers in good condition are also becoming scarce.

An invalid or trembleuse mustache cup would be quite a find! The saucer is made with a protective gate in the center in which the mustache cup sits.

The most sought after treasures are the left-handed mustache cups. According to legend, they were supposed to have been made to order for wives and sweethearts to give to the men returning from the Civil War who had lost the use of their right arms in battle.

INFORMATION FOR THE COLLECTOR

Mustache cups and saucers have been reproduced, and collectors should exercise caution. Left- and right-handed mustache cups marked "Brandenburg" or "JP1200" have turned up regularly during the last 25 years. They usually have a floral transfer with shiny gold trim on the edges and guard. There are also left- and right-handed reproductions marked "R.S. Prussia" and "Nippon."

Collectors should be careful of mismatched mustache cups and saucers, as these "marriages" turn up in the marketplace quite frequently. The value is lower than perfectly matched examples of the same quality.

Because such a large quantity of mustache cups and saucers were made in Germany in the late nineteenth century, many are found with manufacturing defects, such as firing cracks, waving, and little black spots caused by "sputtering" in the second firing. These blemishes are usually acceptable and should never influence a collector to reject an interesting mustache cup and saucer.

Many mustache cups and saucers are unmarked, especially those made in Germany. Others are marked "Germany" or "Made in Germany." A number of mustache cups were made in Japan prior to those marked "Nippon." These lovely and delicate mustache cups were decorated by various family units in small home factories and are unmarked. Mustache cups made in the United States are rarely marked. Those bearing a United States potter's mark are considered quite rare.

Mustache cups are fascinating to collect. At one time practically every household had at least one mustache cup. Today collectors treasure them for their beauty and historical significance.

Soldier drinking cocoa out of mustache cup. Van Houten's Cocoa trade card, c. 1909.

Mustache cup and saucer.

Erdmann Schlegelmilch, Suhl, late nineteenth century.

Bucket-shaped cup with loop handle; hand-painted flowers on cup, brown leaves inside cup and on saucer.

$200.00 – 250.00.

Mustache cup and saucer.

Krister Porcelain Manufactory, Germany, c. 1885.

Slightly scalloped cup, saucer ribbed at rim; pink shaded to white, gilt around edges.

$50.00 – 75.00.

Mustache cup and saucer.

Leuchtemburg (C. A. Lelmann & Sons), Germany, c. 1910 – 1935.

Straight-sided cup with reinforced loop handle; gilded daisies on rim of cup and saucer; water lilies.

$100.00 – 125.00.

Mustache cup and saucer.

Rosenthal, c. 1891 – 1907.

Quatrefoil, very translucent cup and saucer; small purple and blue flowers in each medallion.

$250.00 – 300.00.

Mustache cup and saucer.

Numbered, attributed to R.S. Prussia, c. 1890s.

Cup and saucer in "Drapery" mold, unusual handle; Dainty Floral transfer.

$200.00 – 250.00.

Mustache cup and saucer.

Triple Crown China, Germany, c. 1890s.

Slightly flared and molded cup with rustic handle; lovely rose transfer.

$150.00 – 175.00.

Mustache cup and saucer.

Unmarked, Germany, late nineteenth century.

Scalloped and molded with ornate gilt handle; floral transfer with overpainting.

$80.00 – 100.00.

Mustache cup and saucer.

Unmarked, Germany, c. 1880 – 1910.

Scalloped cup and saucer with unusual handle; ornately molded, inscribed "Present."

$50.00 – 75.00.

Mustache cup and saucer.

Unmarked, Germany, c. 1880 – 1910.

Eight-fluted cup and saucer, ring handle; gilt design on white.

$50.00 – 75.00.

Mustache cup and saucer.

Marked "Made in Germany," c. 1880 – 1910.

Richly encrusted gold floral decoration and beading on pale green luster, inscribed "Forget me not."

$60.00 – 90.00.

Mustache cup and saucer.

Marked "Made in Germany," c. 1880 – 1910.

Ribbed on bottom half of cup and saucer, rope handle, gilt wear on rim.

$50.00 – 65.00.

Mustache cup and saucer.

Unmarked, Germany, c. 1880 – 1910.

Richly decorated with floral sprays and beads on pink luster, ribbed saucer.

$50.00 – 75.00.

Mustache cup and saucer.

Marked "Made in Germany," c. 1880 – 1910.

Richly decorated with floral sprays and beads on pink luster, partially swirled saucer.

$50.00 – 75.00.

Mustache cup and saucer.

Unmarked, Germany, c. 1880 – 1910.

Green luster with interesting stylized floral design with four colorful panels.

$60.00 – 90.00.

Mustache cup and saucer.

Unmarked, Germany, c. 1880 – 1910.

Straight cup with kicked square handle with thumb rest; hand-painted flowers on pale yellow; gilt decoration on lip guard.

$50.00 – 75.00.

Mustache cup and saucer.

Unmarked, Germany, c. 1880 – 1910.

Bucket-shaped cup with square handle; pink luster souvenir cup, "Swing Bridge from Gateshead."

$100.00 – 115.00.

Mustache cup and saucer.

Unmarked, Germany, #4522, c. 1890s.

Heavy cup with decorated ledge, square handle; hand-painted flowers and gilding, molded "Remember Me."

$100.00 – 125.00.

Mustache cup and saucer.

Unidentified mark, probably German, late nineteenth century.

Square quatrefoil can with square handle; hand-painted medallions of flowers, red sponge decoration on blue ground.

$100.00 – 125.00.

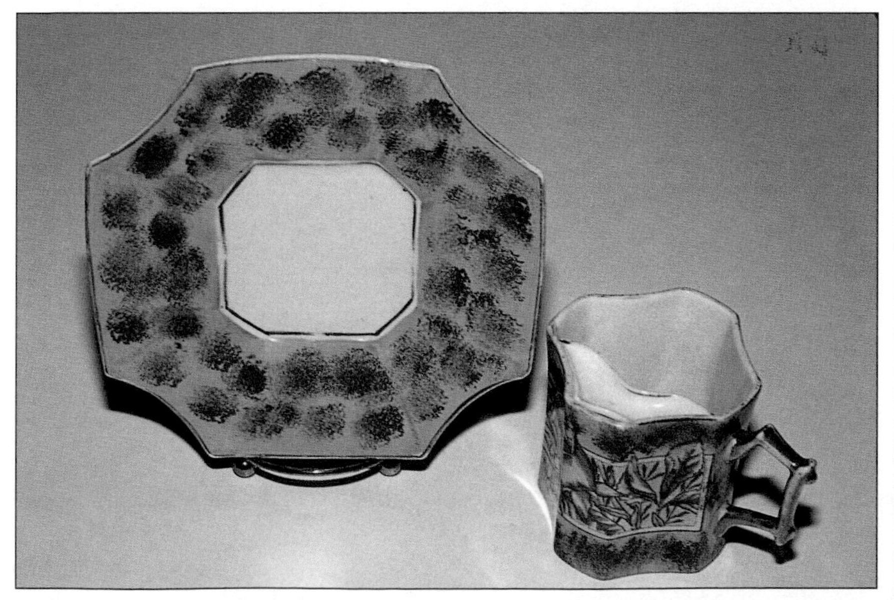

Mustache cup and saucer.

Marked "Germany," c. 1900.

Souvenir cup and saucer with picture of Longfellow's Wayside Inn in Sudbury, Massachusetts (oldest inn in America).

$75.00 – 100.00.

Mustache cup and saucer.

Unmarked, probably German.

Ornately molded cup with wishbone-type handle; white and gold flowers on rose colored ground.

$75.00 – 100.00.

Mustache cup and saucer.

Unmarked, Germany, c. 1890s.

Molded green luster cup with backwards "C" handle; applied forget-me-nots at bottom of cup; "Present."

$75.00 – 100.00.

Mustache cup and saucer.

"Made in Germany," c. 1880s.

Straight cup with rare angel handle; gold leaf decoration with gold "glitter sand."

$125.00 – 150.00.

Close-up of angel handle of above cup.

Mustache cup and saucer.

"Made in Germany," c. 1890 – 1920s.

Rounded cup with loop handle, ribbed saucer; advertising slogan and floral transfer.

$75.00 – 100.00.

Mustache cup and saucer.

Unmarked, c. 1900 – 1930s.

Swirled cup and saucer, coiled handle; yellow leafy design on rim of cup and saucer.

$50.00 – 75.00.

Mustache cup and saucer.

"Made in Germany," c. 1890 – 1920s.

Rounded cup, paneled rim on saucer, squarish handle with thumb rest; applied gilt "Papa," florals, probable saucer mismatch.

$40.00 – 60.00.

Mustache cup and saucer.

Unmarked, Germany, c. 1890s.

Rounded cup with ring handle; applied gold flower and leaves on yellow luster.

$75.00 – 100.00.

Mustache cup and saucer.

Unmarked, Germany, c. 1890s.

Rounded cup with loop handle; hand-painted flowers and "A Present" in gold, blue band on cup and saucer.

$75.00 – 100.00.

Mustache cup and saucer.

Unmarked, Germany, c. 1890s.

Swirled cup and saucer, kidney-shaped handle; attractive gilt decoration.

$75.00 – 100.00.

Mustache cup and saucer.

"Made in Germany," c. 1890 – 1920s.

Straight-sided, six-fluted cup and saucer; flowers and beads separating flutes, "Forget me not."

$75.00 – 100.00.

Mustache cup and saucer.

Union Porcelain Factories, Czechoslovakia, c. 1921 – 1927.

Slightly waisted and scalloped cup with ring handle; colorful rose transfer.

$150.00 – 175.00.

Mustache cup and saucer.

Capodimonte type, c. 1920s.

Rare, left-handed footed cup with fat serpentine handle; star design with cherubs in relief pulling garlands of leaves with colored ornaments.

$175.00 – 225.00.

Mustache cup and saucer.

Limoges, Mc. D. & S., c. 1890 – 1914.

Unusual feather molding on bottom of cup and on saucer; gilt rustic handle; gilt flowers and trim on white.

$175.00 – 225.00.

Mustache cup and saucer.

Limoges, Bawo & Dotter, c. 1880s.

Bucket-shaped cup with curled loop handle; magnificent scenic design with gilt overpainting. (See mark #55.)

$250.00 – 300.00.

Mustache cup and saucer.

Limoges, GDM (Gérard, Dufraisseix, and Morel), dated 1893.

Straight cup with gilt rustic handle; amateur decorated with forget-me-nots on white.

$175.00 – 200.00.

Mustache cup and saucer.

Haviland & Co., made for S. J. R. James (special mark "Feu de Four" added to mark to indicate special firing technique), c. 1876 – 1900.

Round low cup with gilt mustache guard, kicked loop handle; hand-painted roses. (See mark #65.)

$200.00 – 250.00.

Mustache cup and saucer.

Limoges, Unidentified company marked "S & S over L," late nineteenth century.

Swirled cup with rare butterfly guard, swirled saucer; band of decoration on rim, pink inside cup and saucer.

$250.00 – 300.00.

Mustache cup and saucer.

Limoges, Pouyat, Jean, home decorated E. L. M., c. 1891 – 1932.

Eight-paneled rounded cup with aqua rustic handle, scalloped guard; hand-painted flowers.

$150.00 – 200.00.

Mustache cup and saucer.

Limoges, T. & V., home decorated by F. P. Brockway, c. 1892.

Cup tapered at bottom, gilt bamboo type handle with predominant spur; lovely hand-painted pansies. .

$200.00 – 250.00.

Mustache cup and saucer.

French, only marked "300T Depon.," late nineteenth century.

Low cup with pink butterfly handle; hand-painted Autumn leaves.

$250.00 – 275.00.

Mustache cup and saucer.

Nippon, c. 1891 – 1921.

Straight-sided cup with loop handle; scenic with jeweling.

$175.00 – 225.00.

Mustache cup and saucer.

Nippon, c. 1891 – 1921.

Rounded cup with loop handle; garland of hand-painted roses.

$125.00 – 150.00.

Mustache cup and saucer.

Noritake, c. 1911+.

Round cup with floral ledge, loop handle; hand-painted flowers. (See mark #82.)

$150.00 – 175.00.

Mustache cup and saucer.

Japanese, c. 1875 – 1890.

Eight-fluted cup and saucer with heavy ring handle with thumb rest; magnificent hand-enameled flower and ferns, gold beading.

$175.00 – 200.00.

Mustache cup and saucer.

Unmarked, pre-Nippon, c. 1880s.

Paneled cup, wider at bottom; row of hand-painted pink forget-me-nots trimming edge of cup and saucer, much gold on turquoise ground.

$175.00 – 200.00.

Mustache cup and saucer.

Unmarked, pre-Nippon, c. 1880s.

Scalloped cup and foot; wheel and hand-painted flowers and leaf decoration on pink ground.

$150.00 – 175.00.

Mustache cup and saucer.

Bodley, E. J. D., c. 1875 – 1892.

Bucket-shaped cup with magnificent crane handle; yellow with heavily enameled cherry blossoms.

$250.00 – 350.00.

Same cup as above showing full crane.

Mustache cup and saucer.

Aynsley, c. 1930s.

Cup with "D" shaped handle; popular Indian Tree pattern.

$125.00 – 175.00.

Mustache cup and saucer.

Copeland, W. T., c. 1881.

Quatrefoil cup with molded fish scale design at bottom, pinched angular handle; Primrose pattern, rich blue and white. (See mark #21.)

$250.00 – 300.00.

Mustache cup and saucer.

Royal Crown Derby, early 1900s.

Six-panel cup with broken loop handle; Imari pattern.

$250.00 – 300.00.

Mustache cup and saucer.

Hammersley, c. 1939 – 1952.

Large bone china, round cup with loop handle; ducks in flight transfer.

$50.00 – 75.00.

Mustache cup and saucer.

Thomas Poole, Staffordshire, c. 1929 – 1940.

Can with triangular handle; stylized floral transfer.

$75.00 – 100.00.

Mustache cup and saucer.

Gaudy Welsh, c. 1850s.

Straight cup with ring handle; vivid orange and maroon flowers, richly hand gilded.

$175.00 – 200.00.

Mustache cup and saucer.

Wileman & Co. (early Shelley), c. 1897.

Molded cup with loop handle; commemorative celebrating Queen Victoria's 60-year reign.

$300.00 – 350.00.

Breakfast mustache cup and saucer.

Wileman, James, F., c. 1869 – 1892.

Large cup with ring handle (4½"d x 3½"h) and saucer (8"d); Newton pattern. (See mark #116.)

$250.00 – 300.00.

Mustache cup and saucer.

Worcester, c. 1886.

Bucket-shaped cup with bamboo handle; lovely hand-painted flowers.

$300.00 – 350.00.

Mustache cup and saucer.

Unidentified, English Registry mark, c. 1869.

Bucket-shaped cup with turquoise ring handle; enameled blue clovers.

$125.00 – 175.00.

Mustache cup and saucer.

Belleek Pottery Co., c. 1863 – 1890.

Rare Irish Belleek mustache cup and saucer in Grass body shape.

$500.00 – 550.00.

Mustache cup and saucer.

Belleek Pottery Co., c. 1863 – 1890.

Irish Belleek mustache cup and saucer in Shamrock pattern.

$425.00 – 450.00.

Mustache cup and saucer.

Unmarked.

Scalloped cup and saucer, rustic handle; possible reproduction.

$25.00 – 40.00.

Mustache cup and saucer.

Marked "JP1200," probably made in Japan, c. 1960s.

Reproduced left-handed cup and saucer; can also be found decorated with violets or roses.

$50.00 – 60.00.

Mustache cup and saucer.

Quadruple Silver Plate, marked "Poole Silver," c. 1890.

Etched floral design.

$150.00 – 200.00.

Mustache cup and saucer.

Quadruple Plate, marked "Woodman & Cook Co.," c. 1893 – 1914.

Footed cup with fancy scrolled handle; etched flower decoration.

$150.00 – 200.00.

Canterbury dinner service, Syracuse China, Syracuse, New York.

SYRACUSE O.P. CO. CHINA

GOVERNOR WINTHROP SHAPE

Alcora Decoration No. 75501

1 2 - 3 6 - 7 8 - 9 15 - 16 4 - 5

10-11 12-13 14 36

17 18 - 24 25

28 - 29 30

39 26 27 40

42 41

37 - 38 31 - 34 43 - 44

Governor Winthrop shape, Syracuse China, Syracuse, New York.

JOHN AYNSLEY & SONS, LONGTON, Stoke-on-Trent, England.

Albert, A 3194

Coffee Can & Stand, A 3434

Albert A 3410

Albert, A 3500

Venice, 5500

Albert. A 3391

Low Doris, A 3485

Albert, A 3428

Gothic, A 3442

Gothic, A 3164

Albert, A 3513

Low Doris, A 3536

Miscellaneous shapes, c. 1930s, Aynsley China Ltd., Longton, England.

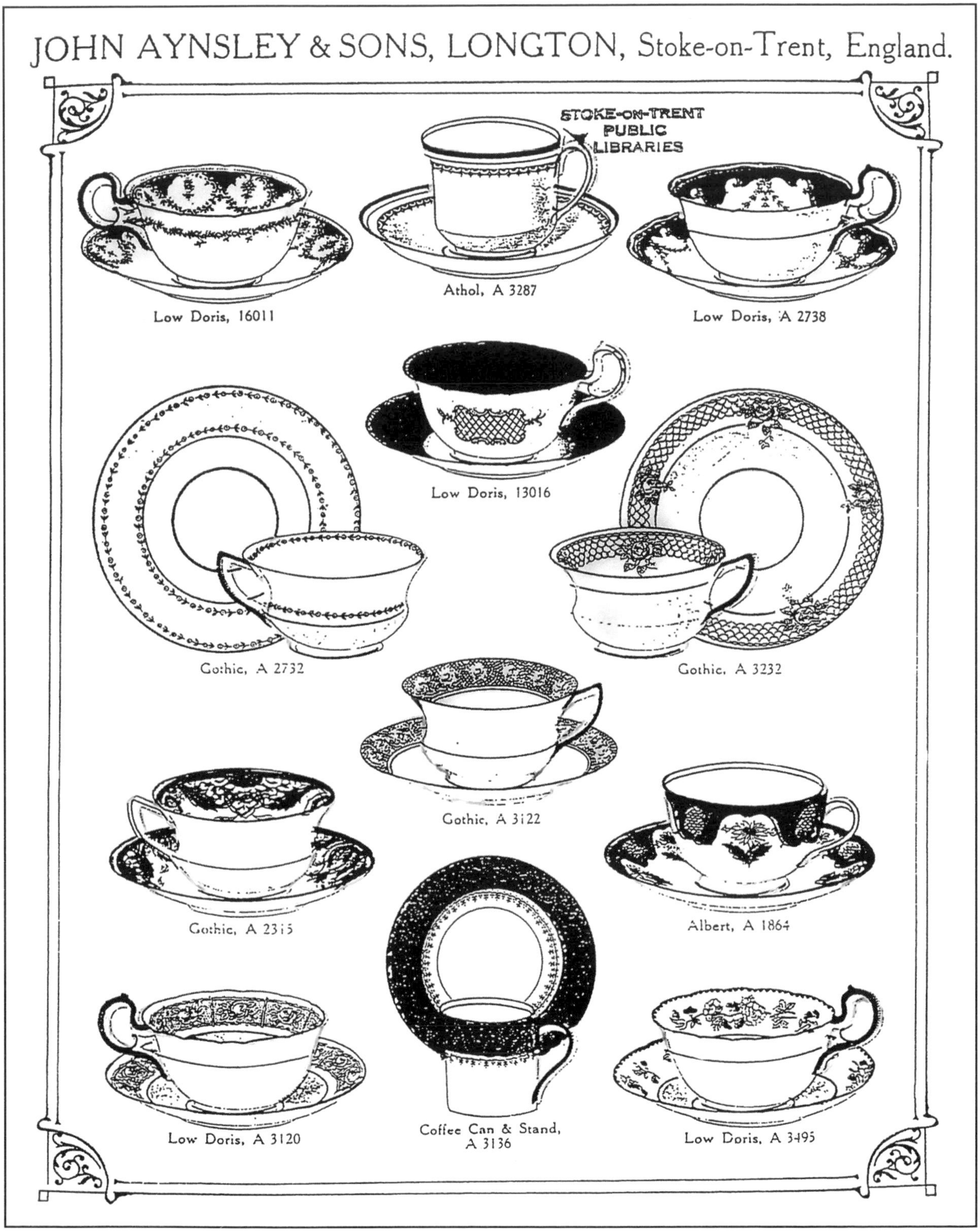
JOHN AYNSLEY & SONS, LONGTON, Stoke-on-Trent, England.
STOKE-ON-TRENT PUBLIC LIBRARIES
Athol, A 3287
Low Doris, 16011
Low Doris, A 2738
Low Doris, 13016
Gothic, A 2732
Gothic, A 3232
Gothic, A 3122
Gothic, A 2315
Albert, A 1864
Low Doris, A 3120
Coffee Can & Stand, A 3136
Low Doris, A 3495

Miscellaneous shapes, c. 1930s, Aynsley China Ltd., Longton, England.

JOHN AYNSLEY & SONS, LONGTON, Stoke-on-Trent, England.

Gothic, A 3255

Albert, A 3520

Gothic, A 3528

Albert, A 3347

Gothic, A 3032

Gothic, A 3462

Coffee Can & Stand, A 3347

Coffee Can & Stand, A 3052

Square B. & B., A 3364

Low Doris, A 3318

Low Doris, A 2846

Albert, A 3364

Miscellaneous shapes, c. 1930s, Aynsley China Ltd., Longton, England.

JOHN AYNSLEY & SONS, LONGTON, Stoke-on-Trent, England.

Gothic, A 3082

Gothic, A 2942

Gothic, A 2929

Gothic, A 3261

Gothic, A 3508

Gothic, A 3285

Coffee Can & Stand, plain, A 3401

B. & B. Plate, A 3357

Coffee Can & Stand, plain, A 2929

Low Doris, A 3186

Early English, A 3357

Gothic, A 3000

Miscellaneous shapes, c. 1930s, Aynsley China Ltd., Longton, England.

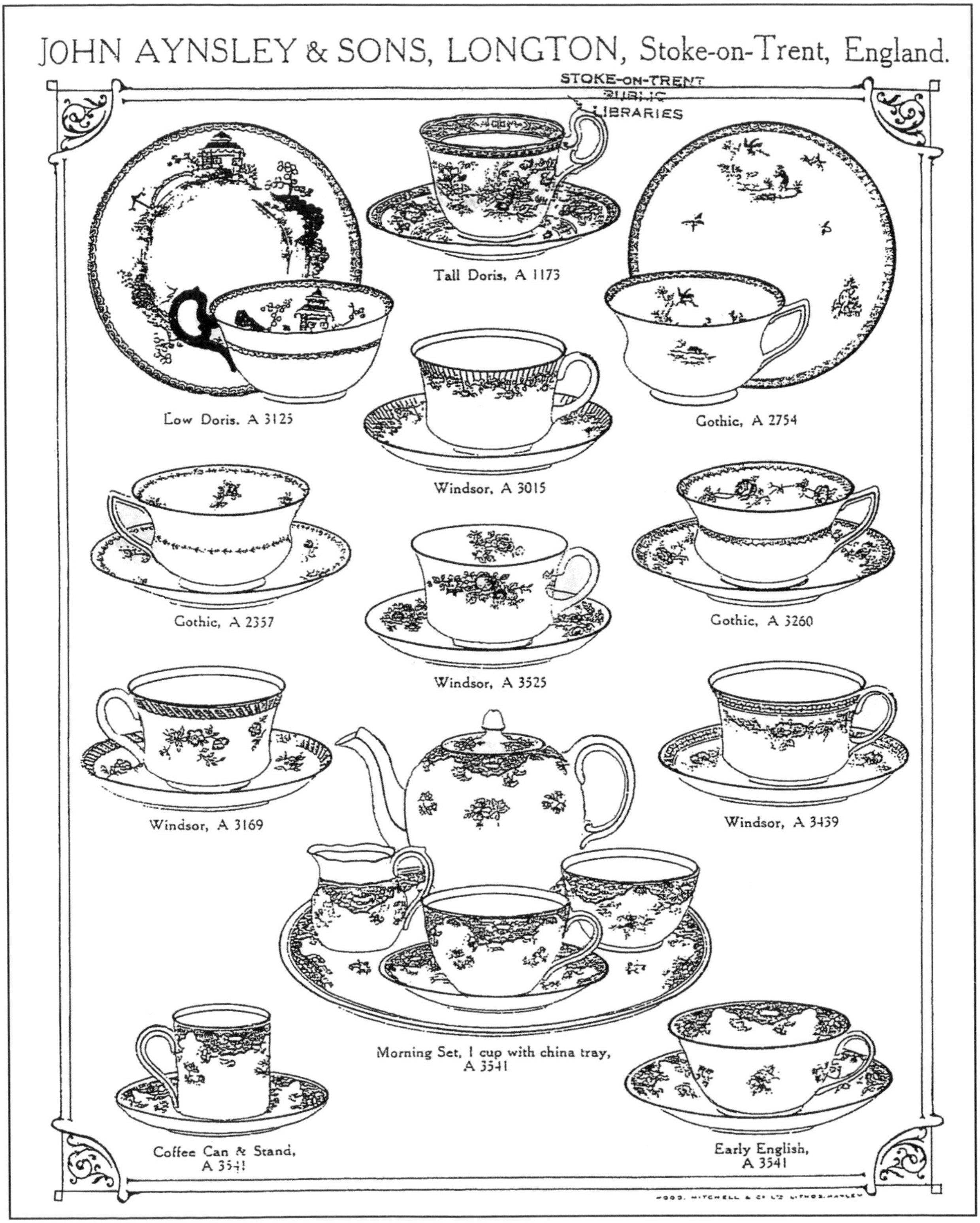

JOHN AYNSLEY & SONS, LONGTON, Stoke-on-Trent, England.

Tall Doris, A 1173

Low Doris, A 3125

Windsor, A 3015

Gothic, A 2754

Gothic, A 2357

Windsor, A 3525

Gothic, A 3260

Windsor, A 3169

Windsor, A 3439

Morning Set, 1 cup with china tray, A 3541

Coffee Can & Stand, A 3541

Early English, A 3541

Miscellaneous shapes, c. 1930s, Aynsley China Ltd., Longton, England.

JOHN AYNSLEY & SONS, LONGTON, Stoke-on-Trent, England.

Athol. A 2746

Albert. A 3329

Albert. A 3471

Tall Doris. A 2052

Albert. A 3464

Albert. A 3504

Coffee Can & Stand, plain
A 3539

Individual Honey,
A 3539

Square B. & B. Plate. A 3539

Albert. A 3539

Early English. A 3539

Breakfast & Saucer, Athol. A 3539

Miscellaneous shapes, c. 1930s, Aynsley China Ltd., Longton, England.

MARKS

1. W. Adams & Sons, Ltd.; Tunstall and Stoke, England, c. 1924.

2. Adderleys Ltd.; Longton, c. 1962+.

3. Charles Ahrenfeldt & Sons; Altrohlau, Bohemia, c. 1886 – 1910.

4. John Aynsley & Sons; Longton, England, c. 1891 – 1920s.

5. John Aynsley & Sons; Longton, England, c. 1920.

6. John Aynsley & Sons; Longton, England, c. 1930s.

7. John Aynsley & Sons; Longton, England, c. 1950s.

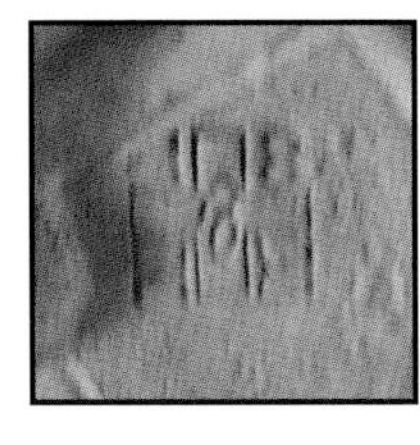

8. Banko Ware; Japan, late nineteenth century.

9. Bing & Grondahl; Copenhagen, Denmark, c. 1948.

10. Bing & Grondahl; Copenhagen, Denmark, c. 1952 – 1958.

11. Brown – Westhead; Moore & Co., Hanley, c. 1890 – 1895.

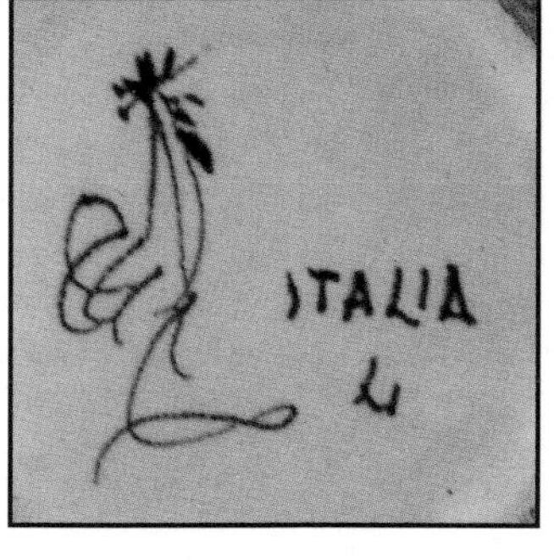

12. Cantagalli, Ulysses; Florence, Italy, c. 1878 – 1901.

13. Carlton Ware, Ltd.; Stoke, England, c. 1920s.

14. Cauldon Ltd.; Hanley, England, c. 1905 – 1920.

15. Coalport Porcelain Works; Shropshire, England, c. 1881 – 1890.

16. Coalport Porcelain Works; Shropshire, England, c. 1891 – 1920.

17. Coalport Porcelain Works; Shropshire, England, c. 1948 – 1950.

18. Coalport Porcelain Works; Shropshire, England, c. 1960 – present.

19. Colclough & Co. (Ridgway Potteries); Stoke, England, c. 1950 – present.

20. Collingwood Bros., Longton, England, c. 1937 – 1957.

21. Copeland, W. T.; Stoke, England, c. 1881.

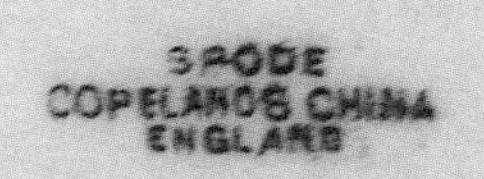

22. Copelands – Spode; Stoke, England, c. 1891+.

23. Crown Staffordshire; Fenton, England, c. 1930s.

24. Crown Staffordshire; Fenton, England, c. 1960s.

25. Crown Derby; Derby, England, c. 1888.

26. Royal Crown Derby; Derby, England, c. 1891.

27. Royal Crown Derby; Derby, England, c. 1907.

28. Royal Crown Derby; Derby, England, c. 1971.

29. Doulton; Burslem, England, c. 1891 – 1902.

30. Royal Doulton, c. 1930s.

31. Dresden, Klemm, R., c. 1888 – 1916.

32. Dresden, Klemm, R., c. 1902 – 1916.

33. Dresden, Lamm, A., c. 1887 – 1891.

34. Dresden, Wissman, c. 1887 – 1890.

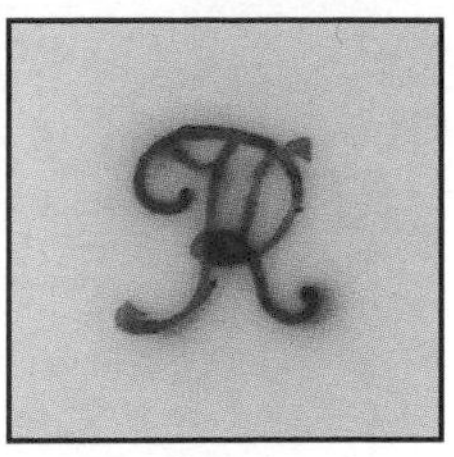

35. Dresden, Wolfsohn, H., c. 1843 – 1883.

36. Dresden, Wolfsohn, H., c. 1886.

37. Elizabethan Fine Bone China; Longton, England, c. 1964 – present.

38. Foley Bone China (E. Brain & Co., Ltd.); Fenton, England, c. 1930 – 1935.

39. Foley Bone China (E. Brain & Co., Ltd.); Fenton, England, c. 1953.

40. Foley Bone China (E. Brain & Co., Ltd.); Fenton, England, c. 1945 – 1963.

41. Hammersley & Co.; Longton, England, c. 1887 – 1912.

42. Hammersley & Co.; Longton, England, c. 1912 – 1939.

43. Hammersley & Co.; Longton, England, c. 1939 – 1950s.

44. Healacraft Bone China; England, c. 1980s.

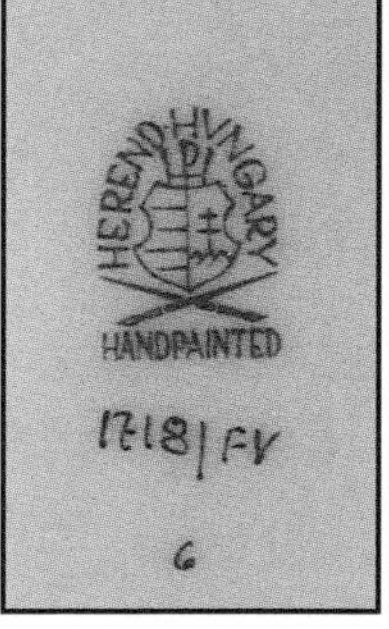

45. Herend; Herend, Hungary, c. 1950s – present.

46. Hudson & Middleton Ltd. (Delphine); Longton, England, c. 1930 – 1946.

47. Hutschenreuther, C. M., Black Knight; Hohenberg, Bavaria, c. 1925 – 1941.

48. Hutschenreuther, L.; Selb, Germany, c. 1887.

49. Hutschenreuther, L.; Selb, Germany, c. 1928 – 1943.

50. Imari, Japan, c. 1900 – 1920.

51. George Jones & Sons; Burslem, England, c. 1890.

52. Josef Kuba; Carlsbad, Germany, c. 1900 – 1945.

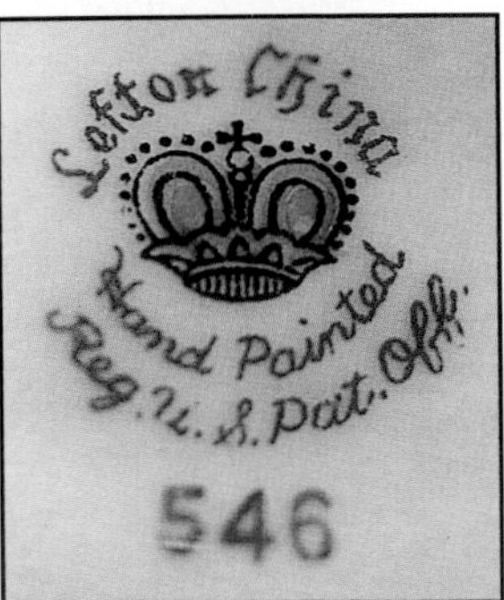

53. Lefton China Co.; Imported to U. S. from Japan, c. 1949 – 1955.

54. Limoges; Ahrenfeldt, C., c. 1894 – 1930.

55. Limoges; Bawo & Dotter, c. 1880s.

56. Limoges; Bawo & Dotter, c. 1920 – 1932.

57. Limoges; Bernardaud & Co., c. 1914 – 1930.

58. Limoges; Coiffe and L. S. & S., c. 1891 – 1914.

59. Limoges; D & Co., decorated by Bernardaud & Co., c. 1900.

60. Limoges; GDA (Gerard, Dufraisseix, & Abbot), c. 1900 – 1941.

61. Limoges; GDM (Gerard, Dufraisseix, & Morel), c. 1882 – 1890.

62. Limoges; Giraud, A., c. 1920s.

63. Limoges; Guerin, c. 1900 – 1932.

64. Limoges; Gutherz, O., c. 1890s.

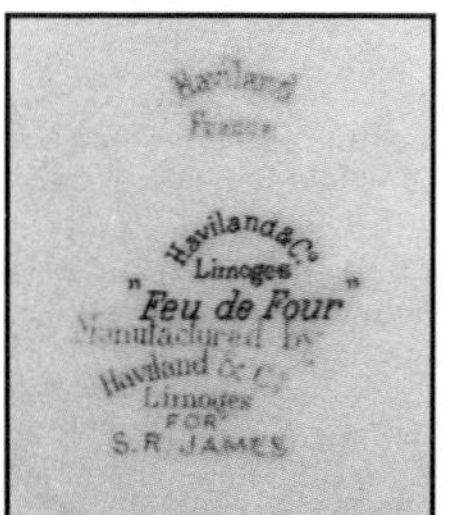

65. Limoges; Haviland & Co., "Feu de Four," c. 1876 – 1900.

66. Limoges; Haviland & Co., c. 1888 – 1896.

67. Limoges; Haviland, Theodore, c. 1893.

68. Limoges; Haviland, Theodore, New York, c. 1937 – present.

69. Limoges; Klingenberg, c. 1890s.

70. Limoges; Leonard exporting mark, c. 1890 – 1914.

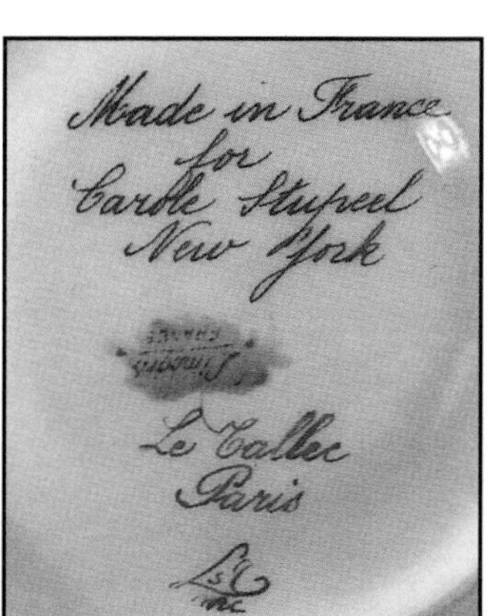

71. Limoges, France, Le Fallec decorating mark, Paris, c. 1930 – 1950.

72. Limoges; Pouyat, J., c. 1914 – 1932.

73. Limoges; Redon, M., c. 1882 – 1896.

74. Limoges; Tressemann & Vogt, c. 1892 – 1907.

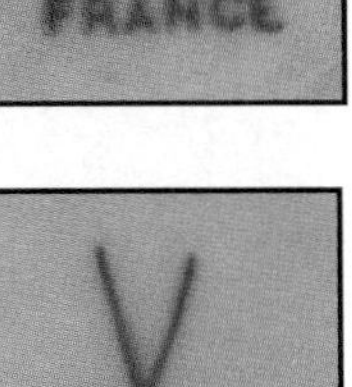

75. Meissen (States Porcelain Manufactory); Meissen, Germany, c. 1860 – 1924.

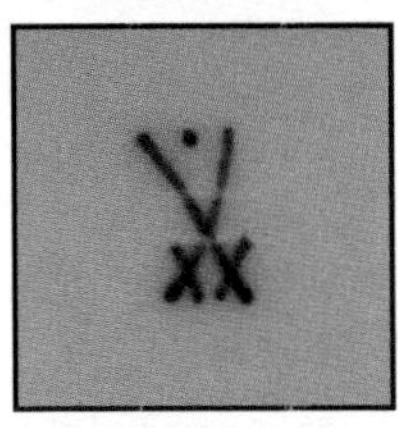

76. Meissen (States Porcelain Manufactory); Meissen, Germany, second choice, c. 1924 – 1934.

77. Minton; Stoke, England, c. 1912 – 1950.

78. Minton; Stoke, England, c. 1951 – present.

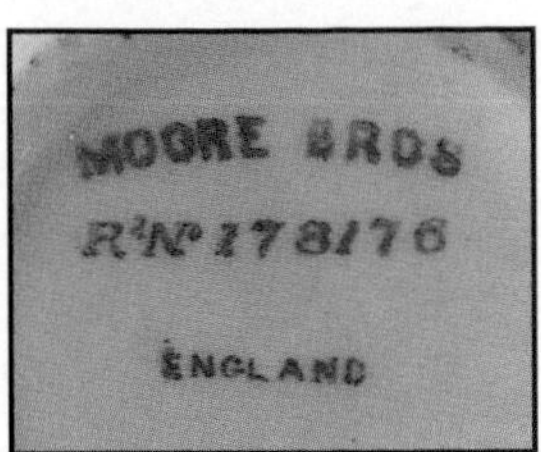

79. Moore Brothers; Longton, England, c. 1891.

80. M.Z. Austria (Moritz Zdekauer); Altrohlau, Bohemia, c. 1900.

81. Myott, Son & Co.; Staffordshire, England, c. 1930+.

82. Noritake, Japan, c. 1911+.

83. Nymphenburg (Royal Porcelain Manufactory); Nymphenburg, Germany, c. 1895.

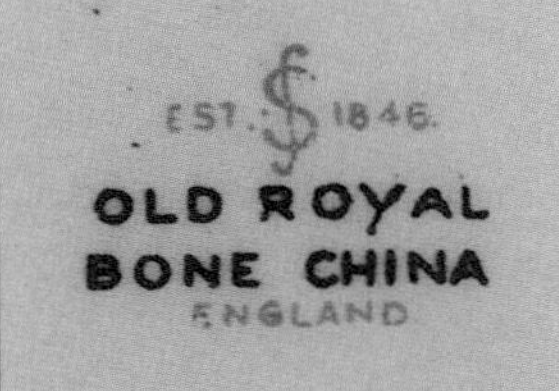

84. Old Royal Bone China (Samson Smith); Longton, England, c. 1930 – 1941.

85. Paragon China Co. Ltd.; Longton, c. 1939 – 1949.

86. Paragon China Co. Ltd.; Longton, c. 1957+.

87. Persian Ware (unidentified maker); Germany, c. 1930s.

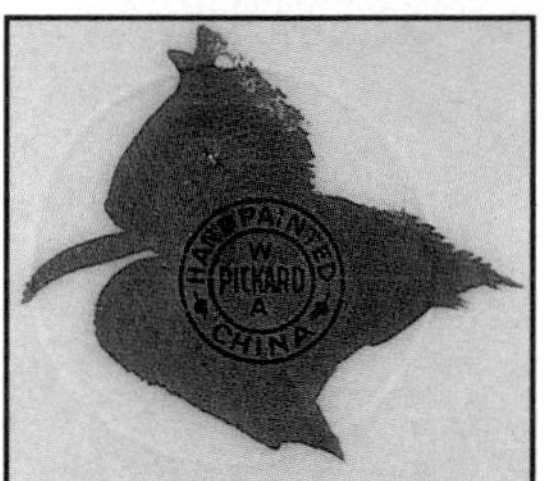

88. Pickard, W.; Chicago, Illinois, c. 1912 – 1918.

89. Samuel Radford Ltd.; Fenton, England, c. 1938 – 1957.

90. Regency China Ltd.; Longton, England, c. 1953 – present.

91. Rosenthal; Selb, Bavaria, c. 1901 – 1933.

92. Rosenthal Studio Line; Selb, Bavaria, c. 1950s.

93. Rosina China Co. Ltd.; Longton, England, c. 1946 – 1948.

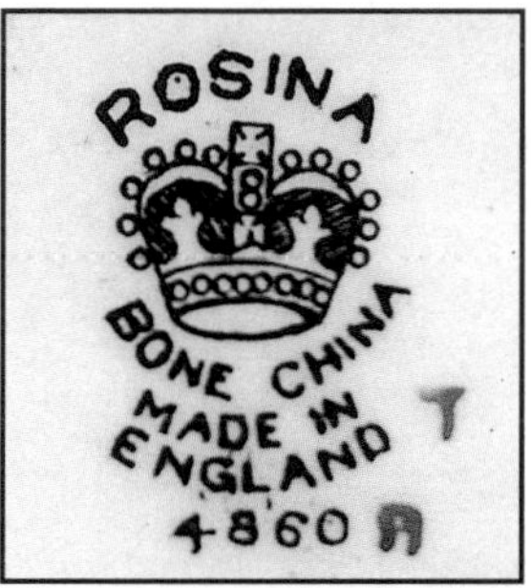

94. Rosina China Co. Ltd.; Longton, England, c. 1952+.

95. Royal Albert (Thomas C. Wild & Sons); Longton, England, c. 1934.

96. Royal Albert (Thomas C. Wild & Sons); Longton, England, c. 1945 – present.

97. Royal Albert (Thomas C. Wild & Sons); Longton, England, current mark.

98. Royal Bayreuth (Porcelain Factory Tettau); Tettau, Germany, c. 1902.

99. Royal Copenhagen Porcelain Factory; Copenhagen, Denmark, c. 1922 – present.

100. Royal Dover; England, current mark.

101. Royal Kent (James Kent, Ltd.); Longton, England, current mark.

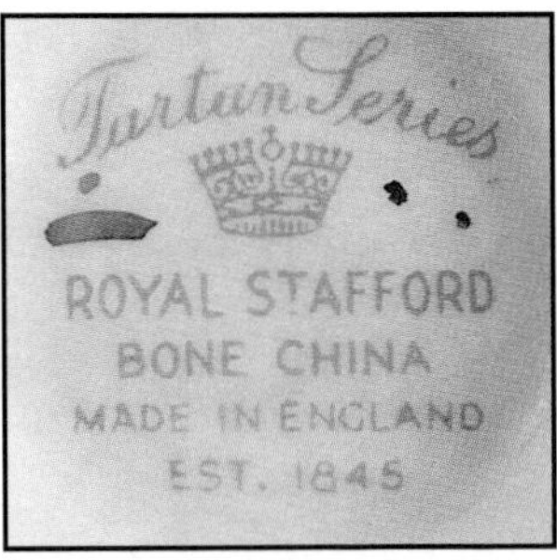

102. Royal Stafford China; Longton, England, c. 1952 – present.

103. Royal Standard (Chapmans Longton Ltd.); Longton, England, c. 1949 – present.

104. Royal Sutherland (Hudson & Middleton Ltd.), c. 1947 – 1959.

105. R.S. Prussia (Reinhold Schlegelmilch); Suhl, Germany, c. 1904 – 1938.

106. Von Schierholz's Porcelain Manufactory; Plaue, Germany, c. 1907.

107. Schumann, Carl; Arzberg, Germany, c. 1918 – 1929.

108. Schumann, Carl; Arzberg, Germany, c. 1932.

109. Schumann, Carl; Arzberg, Germany, current mark.

110. Shelley Potteries Ltd.; Longton, England, c. 1925 – 1940.

111. Societa Ceramica Richard; Milan, Italy (Capodimonte), c. 1930 – present.

112. Societa Ceramica Richard; Milan, Italy (Ginori), current mark.

113. Societe de Faiencerie de Salens; France, c. 1868 – 1880.

114. Taylor & Kent Ltd.; Longton, England, c. 1939 – 1949.

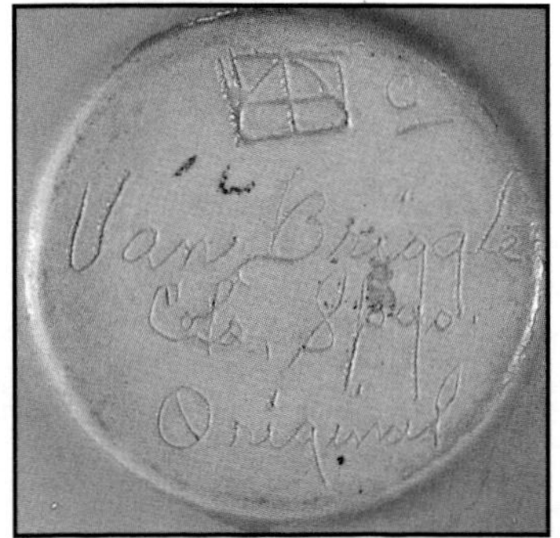

115. Van Briggle; Colorado Springs, Colorado, c. 1950s.

116. Wileman, James, F. (early Shelley); Longton, England, c. 1869 – 1992.

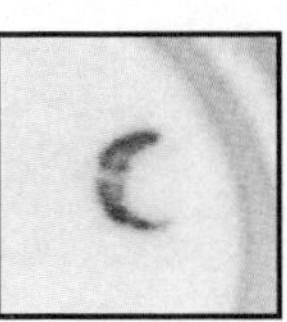

117. Worcester; Worcester, England (filled-in crescent mark), c. 1755 – 1790.

118. Chamberlin Worcester; Worcester, England, c. 1840 – 1850.

119. Worcester; Worcester, England, c. 1875.

120. Royal Worcester; Worcester, England, c. 1927.

121. Royal Worcester; Worcester, England, c. 1944 – 1955.

122. Royal Worcester; Worcester, England, c. 1950s.

BIBLIOGRAPHY

Ashby, H. K. *Cocoa, Tea & Coffee*. New York, New York: Crane, Russak & Company Inc., 1977.

Bagdade, Susan and Al. *Warman's American Pottery and Porcelain*. Radnor, Pennsylvania: Wallace-Homestead Book Co., 1994.

____. *Warman's English and Continental Pottery and Porcelain*. Radnor, Pennsylvania: Wallace-Homestead Book Co., 1991.

____. *Warman's English and Continental Pottery and Porcelain*. Iola, Wisconsin: Krause Publications, 1998.

Banner, Mannie. "Shelley: Potters to the World Part 2-4." *Antique Trader*, 1/21/98, 3/18/98, 6/10/98.

Battie, David. *Guide To Understanding 19th and 20th Century British Porcelain*. Wappingers Falls, New York: Antique Collector's Club, 1994.

Bergesen, Victoria. *Bergesen's Price Guide to British Ceramics*. London, England: Barrie and Jenkins, 1992.

Berthoud, Michael. *A Compendium of British Cups*. Bridgnorth, Shropshire, England: Micawber Publications, 1990.

Boger, Louise Ade. *The Dictionary of World Potters and Porcelain*. New York, New York: Charles Scribner's & Sons, 1971.

Carter, Tina M. *Teapots*. Philadelphia, Pennsylvania: Courage Books, 1995.

Clark, Garth. *The Book of Cups*. New York, New York: Cross River Press, 1990.

Colley, Edith. "Tea Time." *Hobbies*, 6/47.

Cushion, John. *An Illustrated Dictionary of Ceramics*. New York, New York: Von Nostrand Reinhold Company, 1974.

Davis, Howard. *Chinoiserie: Polychrome Decoration of Staffordshire Porcelain 1790 – 1850*. London, England: Rublicon Press, 1991.

Degenhardt, R. K. *Belleek — The Complete Collector's Guide and Illustrated Reference*. Huntington, New York: Portfolio Press, 1993.

Eberle, Linda and Scott, Susan. *The Charlton Standard Catalogue of Chintz, 2nd Edition*. Birmingham, Michigan: The Charlton Press, 1997.

Emmerson, Robin. *One for the Pot, British Teapots and Tea Drinking*. Norwich, England: Twining Teapot Gallery at Norwich Castle Museum.

Fehrenbacker, Jane and Fox, Carolyn. "The Chintz Collector." *Antique Trader*, 9/97.

Field, Rachael. *Buying Antique Pottery and Porcelain*. Radnor, Pennsylvania: Wallace-Homestead Book Co., 1987.

Freeman, John Crosby. *Victorian Entertaining*. Philadelphia, Pennsylvania: Running Press, 1989.

Frelinghuysen, Alice Cooney. *American Porcelain 1770 – 1920*. New York, New York: The Metropolitan Museum of Art, 1989.

Forrest, Tim. Consulting Editor, Paul Atterbury. *The Bullfinch Anatomy of Antique China and Silver*. New York, New York: Little, Brown and Company, 1998.

Gaston, Mary Frank. *The Collector's Encyclopedia of R. S. Prussia*. Paducah, Kentucky: Collector Books, 1982.

____. *The Collector's Encyclopedia of Limoges Porcelain*. Paducah, Kentucky: Collector Books, 1980.

Gluck, Nancy. "The Golden Touch of Pickard Studios China." *AntiqueWeek*, 11/25/96.

Godden, Geoffrey. *Encyclopedia of British Pottery and Porcelain Marks*. London, England: Barrie & Jenkins, 1986, 1991.

____. *Godden's Guide to English Porcelains*. Radnor, Pennsylvania: Wallace-Homestead Book Co., 1978, 1992.

____. *Godden's Guide to European Porcelains*. London, England: Cross River Press, 1993.

Grosvenor Marketing, Ltd. "The Art of Tea Drinking and Tea Related Artifacts Preserved by Twinings." *Antique and Auction News*, 11/98.

Halperin, Lynn. "He Collects Mustache Cups." *Hobbies*, 5/52.

Hammon, Dorothy. *Mustache Cups*. Des Moines, Iowa: Wallace-Homestead Book Co., 1972.

Harran, Jim and Susan. *Collectible Cups and Saucers, Identification & Values*. Paducah, Kentucky: Collector Books, 1997.

Helm, Peter. Geoffrey Godden, Editor. "The Hilditch Porcelains, c. 1811 – 1867." *Staffordshire Porcelains*. Granada Publishing, 1983.

Holgate, David. *New Hall*. Faber & Faber, 1987.

Holt, Geraldene. *A Cup of Tea*. London, England: Pavilion Ltd., 1991.

Huxford, Sharon and Bob. *Schroeder's Antiques Price Guide, 17th edition*. Paducah, Kentucky: Collector Books, 1999.

Joseph, Francis. *Collecting Carlton Ware*. London, England: Francis Joseph Publishers, 1994.

Kamm, Dorothy. "Soups On." *Porcelain Collector's Companion*, 12/98.

____. "Designing Women." *Antique Trader Weekly*, 9/95.

Kovel, Ralph and Terry. *Know Your Antiques*. New York, New York: Crown Publishers, Inc., 1967.

____. *Kovels' Antiques and Collectibles Price List*. New York, New York: Three Rivers Press, 1998.

____. *Kovels' New Dictionary of Marks*. New York, New York: Crown Publishers, Inc., 1986.

Long, Delores M. "Genesis of the Snack Set." *Antique & Auction News*, 7/18/97.

Mackay, James. *An Encyclopedia of Small Antiques*. New York, New York: Harper and Row, 1975.

McGrath, Wendy, "Shelley China." *Antiques & Collecting Magazine*. Chicago, Illinois: Dale K. Graham, December 1995.

Messenger, Michael. *Coalport 1795 – 1926*. Woodbridge, Suffolk, England: Antique Collectors Club, 1995.

Miller, Judith. *Miller's Antiques Encyclopedia*. London, England: Reed Consumer Books Ltd., 1998.

Norman, Barbara. *Tales of the Table*. Englewood Cliffs, New Jersey: Prentice-Hall, 1972.

Palmer, Marcia L. "Comparing and Contrasting Chinese and English Tea Ware." *Internet: http://www.stashtea.com/teaware.html*.

Ray, Marcia. *Collectible Ceramics*. New York, New York: Crown Publishers, 1974.

Reed, Alan B. *Collector's Encyclopedia of Pickard China*. Paducah, Kentucky: Collector Books, 1995.

Rogers, Connie. "Is It Old Or New? Know Before You Buy Willow Pattern China." *AntiqueWeek*, 3/16/98.

Röntgen, Robert E. *Marks on German, Bohemian & Austrian Porcelain*. Exton, Pennsylvania: Schiffer Publishing Ltd., 1981.

____. *The Book of Meissen*. Exton, Pennsylvania: Schiffer Publishing Ltd., 1984.

Rust, Gordon A. *Collector's Guide to Antique Porcelain*. New York, New York: The Viking Press, 1973.

Saks, Bill. "Studying English Ceramics." *Antique Trader*, 6/12/96.

Sandon, Henry. *Coffee Pots and Teapots for the Collector*. New York, New York: Arco Publishing Company, Inc., 1974.

Sandon, John. *Antique Porcelain*. Woodbridge, Suffolk, England: Antique Collector's Club, 1997.

Scott, Susan. "Chintz." *Antique Trader*, 9/20/95.

____. "Ladies of the Pottery." *Antique Journal*, 9/93.

____. "Collecting Chintz." *Today's Collector*, 5/97.

____. "A. G. Richardson Crown Ducal Chintz." *Antique Trader Weekly*, 10/30/96.

Sikota, Gyözö. *Herend — The Art of Hungarian Porcelain*. New York, New York: Püski Publishing, 1989.

Smith, Michael. *The Afternoon Tea Cook*. Collier Macmillan Canada, Inc., 1986.

Timm, Maureen. "Historic Mottoware From Torquay." *Antique Trader Weekly*, 2/7/96.

Twitchett, John and Bailey, Betty. *Royal Crown Derby*. London, England: Antique Collectors Club Ltd., 1976.

Ware, George. *German and Austrian Porcelain*. New York, New York: Crown Publishers, Inc., 1963.

Wenzel, Lynn. "Collectors Love the Artistry of Rosenthal." *AntiqueWeek*, 2/23/98.

____. *The Archives*, Syracuse China Company, P. O. Box 4820, Syracuse, New York 13221.

____. *Aynsley China Limited*, Portland Works, Longton, England ST31HS.

____. "Coffee Universe-ity." *Internet: http://www.coffeeuniverse.com/university_hist.html*.

____. "History of China Manufacturers, Discontinued China." *Internet: http://www.discontinuedchina.com*.

____. "The History of Tea." *Internet: http://sameoldgrind.com/teahist.html*.

____. *Illustrated World Encyclopedia*, Vol. 19. Bodley Publishing Corp., 1965.

____. *The Lorenz Hutschenreuther Fine China Brevier*. Selb, Germany: Porzellanfabriken Hutschenreuther.

____. Pickard China Company, 872 Pickard Avenue, Antioch, Illinois 60002-1574.

____. "Some of Our Favorite Quotes" and "Tea Facts." The Stash Tea Company, 1966 – 1998. *Internet: http://www.stashtea.com/quotes.html*.

____. *"The Story of Minton."* Stoke-on-Trent, England: Royal Doulton Tableware, Ltd., 1978.

____. *Victoria The Charms of Tea*. Compiled by the editors of *Victoria* magazine. New York, New York: The Hearst Corp., 1991.

INDEX

D

E

F

G

H

INDEX

INDEX